from
PRAIRIE ROOTS
to
LAKE ERIE SHORES

MY STORY IN MY WORDS

JOAN HARDER

◆ FriesenPress

One Printers Way
Altona, MB R0G 0B0
Canada

www.friesenpress.com

Copyright © 2022 by Joan Harder
First Edition — 2022

Cover Art "Memories" by Janet E Thomas
Cover Art Photographer, Marianne Kovacs
Editors, Janet E Thomas and John C Thomas

All rights reserved.

No part of this publication may be reproduced in any form, or by any means, electronic or mechanical, including photocopying, recording, or any information browsing, storage, or retrieval system, without permission in writing from FriesenPress.

ISBN
978-1-03-916821-3 (Hardcover)
978-1-03-916820-6 (Paperback)
978-1-03-916822-0 (eBook)

1. BIOGRAPHY & AUTOBIOGRAPHY, PERSONAL MEMOIRS

Distributed to the trade by The Ingram Book Company

To my family and dear friends

Joan Harder

The Image of Me

I have gazed into the mirror and the face that looks at me
is a face that's seen a lot of life. I hope there's more to see.
But inside, I'm climbing mountains, swimming rivers,
fishing streams,
holding babies, loving lovers, making plans to fulfill dreams.
Don't you know that what you see is just a carton holding Me?
Slightly ragged on the edges, torn in spots and losing shape,
but it's me. I am still in there, when you see me don't just gape.
I'm a daughter, giggling school girl, then a fiancée and wife,
then a mother, teaching babies how to navigate through life.
And throughout this life there is the wondrous joy of friends
making every day much better. Oh, I hope that never ends.
And late at night, when I'm in bed, reality creeps in,
listens as I say a prayer, tucks my quilt beneath my chin,
and as my eyes close sleepily I just can't help but grin!

Joan Harder

My Prairie Roots: Altario, Provost, and Stettler

The little town of Altario, Alberta, where I lived for the first six years of my life, was just that, little. Perched literally in the middle of nowhere, and like so many prairie towns, identifiable only by the familiar grain elevators which seemed to soar over the smattering of houses, their height matched only by the spire of the Catholic Church. There were a few stores, a post office, hardware and lumber yard, a café run by Chinese brothers Wing and Wong, a hotel, community hall, livery barn, a repair garage and perched on a rise on the edge of town, the one-room school and teacherage. Of course every town had a railway station. Across the tracks from that was the section house, always painted a familiar color that everyone called "CPR red." Whoever sold that paint must have been wealthy because the countryside was dotted with barns, outhouses and sheds of that same familiar color. It was enduring though, withstanding harsh winters as well as the hot, windy summers which were bill of fare in east central Alberta during the 30's.

It was there, in Altario, that my dad Clifford Thomas met my mom Mildred Louise McLeod. Cliff worked on a farm, owned a garage in Altario and then sold farm machinery. Mildred graduated from Camrose Normal School and was a teacher in the district for a short time. My parents married in 1927 after a brief courtship. At the time their union was not popular with my mother's family. I've never really known why, but I do know the problem resolved over time.

My father Cliff was born in Wales to David and Kate Thomas December 8, 1903. In 1912 he, his mother and older sister Alice immigrated to Canada to join David, who was already employed as a carpenter. After working on CPR construction in British Columbia the family moved to Calgary and then in 1917 to Altario.

Cliff, Kate, David and Alice in BC after their arrival in Canada

Grandma Mame with her kids, L to R my mom Millie, Aunty Ruby, Aunt Meatie and Uncle Jack.

My mother's parents Duncan W. McLeod and Mame Cordick were born in Bruce County, Ontario. Three of their children were born there: my mom Mildred Louise, Marguerite (Meatie) and John Alexander (Jack). About 1913 they left Ontario and settled on a farm just south of Altario. Their youngest child Ruby Estelle was born in Altario hospital.

I don't remember my two sets of grandparents being terribly friendly with each other.

Grandma Thomas had an air of grandeur about her, which my grandpa didn't share. Both of them came from hard working coal mining families in Wales. Since Grandma and Grandpa McLeod were very down to earth folks and held no illusions about themselves, this very likely was the reason they were never close. Grandma Thomas rather ran the show at their house, and Papa (that was what we called Grandpa Thomas) usually went along with this, only rebelling on occasion.

The Sky-Ooflam for the Hootabloo

My papa, David Dorward Thomas, was probably the most memorable character of my childhood. Born in a coal mining district of Wales, he married his childhood sweetheart, Kate Higgins. To each other they were Dave and Kit. My big brother Davey (three years older than me) and I thought it was really funny that Grandma's name was the same as that of a comic strip character of the time, Kitty Higgins.

Papa and Grandma Thomas

They were an oddly matched couple. Grandma was quite tall and portly, while Papa was shorter and quite slight in build. They were as different in personality as they were in appearance. Grandma always gave the impression of someone who had quite possibly married beneath herself. Papa had no airs and, no matter what Grandma's ideas were, he refused to rise to her expectations.

By today's standards Papa would be considered pretty well dressed. His uniform was rumpled wool trousers, held up on his slight frame by suspenders. His shirt was usually white with stripes, over which he wore a vest. The always-too-long sleeves of his shirt were held back with armbands just above the elbow. This created a puffed look that always made me think of the comic character Popeye. However, instead of Popeye's pipe, my papa always had a cigarette dangling precariously from his bottom lip, with at least a half inch of ash ready to drop at any moment. I was fascinated by that ash.

I stared, hypnotized, waiting breathlessly for it to fall. Come to think of it, one could probably have found my papa just by following his trail of ashes. Sometimes he rolled the cigarette on his tongue until it tilted upward and then he blew, squinting his eyes as ashes scattered. He wore glasses that were generally dotted with specks of sawdust. Fingers of his calloused hands were yellowed with nicotine. I doubt there was a time when at least two of his fingernails weren't blackened from an errant hammer, the tool of his trade. He was a cabinet maker and a finishing carpenter and he was my hero.

I loved to spend hours hovering around him as he worked in the shop attached to the post office. He was postmaster but his real love was woodworking. He could build a house or a finely tooled tea cart with hundreds of tiny pieces of inlaid wood. He spent countless hours sanding, varnishing and patiently rubbing a finish until it glowed like fine satin and felt the same. When he was finished he took my hand and ran it over the smooth wood, waiting for words he knew would come. "Oh, Papa, it's just like glass!" He'd grin with pride. However, his patience was limited when he was engrossed in a new job. When his familiar whistle began to sound more like a hiss and blew ashes from his ever present cigarette, it was time to go.

Often, as Papa worked, Davey and I helped ourselves to small pieces of unused wood, busily hammering away on our own creations. We knew better than to dip into the nail bucket but there were plenty of slightly bent ones lying in the sawdust on the floor. As long as we stayed well out of the way of Papa's saw, and didn't ask too many questions, everything went just fine.

We were used to hearing Papa turn the air blue with curses when the hammer slipped and caught his finger instead of a nail. Occasionally, we experimented with some of these choice words ourselves, out of his earshot, of course. We felt like real grown-ups shouting the odd "dammit" or "Jesus Christ" or, better still, the all-time favorite "God damn it to Hell" saved for particularly critical times.

One thing always puzzled us. We didn't know the names of the pieces Papa crafted. They all looked different, but when we asked, "Papa what are you making today?" his reply was always the same.

He took his cigarette out of this mouth and without looking up from his work he said, "I'm making a skyooflam for the 'ootabloo." His Welsh brogue automatically dropped the "h."

Somehow, even though that left us puzzled, we never pressed for a better explanation. It was as though, by leaving us with that, we would remain happily mystified and slightly in awe of what went on in that dusty smoky shop. And we were sure to come back again tomorrow.

The Penny

The other day my friend and I were crossing the street when I spied a penny on the pavement. I thought it a bit strange as pennies were no longer in circulation but as is the custom, I handed it to my friend and wished her luck. Then I noticed it was an American one cent piece. Seeing that, I put it out of my mind, or so I thought.

Later, at home, I remembered that penny and my thoughts slipped back to my childhood. Davey and I were lucky to live next door to our papa. My papa, the postmaster, was always busy. When he wasn't getting mail bags ready for the train or sorting letters into boxes next to the wicket, he was in his workshop in the back. He enjoyed being a postmaster and he said it meant a regular salary. But cabinet making was what he loved to do. *Sitting in my chair at home today, I can almost smell smoke from Papa's ever-present cigarette mixed with the aroma of newly sawed wood, fresh shavings lying in curls, and the pungent odor of glue. All were such a part of him.*

Davey

We knew Papa liked having us around but if we touched the wrong tool or broke something, his language sent us scurrying home. He never laid a hand on us but the stream of cursing was enough to "scare the beJesus" out of us. We did try hard to please him. Unless we were really in trouble, we knew at some point he would reach into the pocket of his baggy wool trousers and, as though we didn't know what was coming, he would put out both his closed hands and ask us to choose one. I don't know why we always acted surprised.

Without fail, each hand held a shiny copper penny. Off we'd go up the street to the little Red and White Store to buy our favorite candy. It was a dark day when Papa didn't give us pennies and, if it did happen, we tried to be especially good for the rest of the day.

Mom always knew we were in trouble with Papa when we'd hang around the house. She pried it out of us eventually and somehow, in her quiet way, managed to make us feel bad. Off we went to tell Papa, "Sorry."

But if that didn't work we went to see what treats Grandma had, especially if she knew Papa had sent us packing. It seemed Grandma didn't miss much. As a matter of fact, sometimes it was hard to tell who really was postmaster because Grandma seemed to be the real boss in the family. I overheard Mama say she kept a "tight hand on the purse strings" but Grandma didn't seem to mind when Papa handed us those big copper pieces of old. They were so precious to me. The penny was a bit larger than a quarter and felt so warm in my hand. Davey said they weren't worth nearly as much as a quarter, nevertheless, I felt rich.

Funny how such a little thing as a penny should stir up memories, scents and feelings from another time. For a while I felt sad because they are just memories, and you know, I really miss those pennies.

The Washing Machine

I think I was four, so it must have been 1936 when Grandma Thomas had her incident with the washing machine.

I was doing my favorite job for Papa. As I've said, Papa was a smoker of grand proportion. He even invented his own cigarette rolling machine and to this day I have never seen another like it. There was a real trick to making the perfect product. I learned that too tight or too loose earned a string of Papa's all too familiar obscenities, but swearing was such a part of Papa, that "God dammit to hell" only caused me to cringe slightly. After all, I could have torn open the offending cigarette and reused the tobacco. But it was the 30's and, although little packets of papers cost only a few cents, it was money not easily come by. Especially for something as frivolous as smokes (Grandma's opinion, not Papa's). I had managed to make quite an imposing pile of nicely packed ones, and now was busily snipping off bits of tobacco that hung out the ends of the white tubes.

Grandma was doing a load of washing on the porch, just off the kitchen where I sat. She had the very most up to date machine there was at the time, electric, with an automatic wringer.

As my mother had let slip in my hearing, Grandma controlled the money in the Thomas household. (I didn't realize how rare that was until much later.) She managed nicely to have things that allowed her to hold what she believed was an important place in the social strata of our town. Papa turned his earnings over to Grandma who, in turn, gave him a small amount of spending money for cigarette makings and sometimes beer at the local beer parlour. This last expenditure never quite seemed in Grandma's character. I suspect that somewhere early in their marriage a younger, tougher Papa convinced her that it was in her best interest to allow him some small pleasures, even if it was done grudgingly.

This particular day, Grandma's wonderful washing machine, much admired by the town's ladies, was purring and whining its way through a wash load. All seemed well with the world.

A high pitched screech changed that in the space of a second. Something terrible had happened on the porch. By the time I got there, Grandma was spread-eagled across the top of the washer with her feet off the floor and hands firmly gripping each end of the wringer. Her eyes rolled back in her head and between screeches she cried, "Papa! Get Papa!"

I had no idea what had happened, but there was no doubt it was serious. I ran out the door toward Papa's shop yelling at the top of my lungs. When I was halfway there Papa appeared at the door, grabbed his cap and started running. "What the hell is all the fuss? Where's your Grandma?" he panted. He left me in the dust as he headed for the house.

By the time I got there, Grandma was sprawled half-sitting on the porch floor sobbing, cradling her ample bosom in her arms, rocking back and forth as though comforting a baby. The washer was strangely quiet. Papa gingerly patted Grandma on the shoulder.

"What happened, what's wrong?" I was surprised at how my voice shook, and suddenly, my knees collapsed and I dropped to the floor beside Grandma. Papa picked me up and took me to the kitchen where he put me on a chair. Then he went back to the porch where Grandma's sobs had subsided to lower moans and sniffles.

There was some muttering and though I strained to hear, just one or two words made sense, "Not to know…laughing stock…You hear me, Dave?"

Well, somehow, things settled down. Papa put the kettle on for a cuppa. I had lots of questions to ask, but the look on Grandma's face made me think better of it. Besides, Papa put my tea in a saucer, added lots of sugar and blew it 'til it was cool. I was content to drink it noisily, somehow sure no one would really care about manners today.

That was all I knew until the next day. I overheard Grandma recounting in detail to my Mom how she'd caught her left breast in the wonderful automatic wringer while she tried to unstick a sock that was caught up and wound around. The wringer just kept on going and going and going. Oh, yes, she was quite bruised, she exclaimed, "Look here, I'll be such a mess!" And Mama, my gentle mama, assured her that it would soon be much better and no one needed to know any more about it.

Oh, I would have given a lot to have seen those bruises, especially on Grandma, whose chest jiggled a lot more than other ladies I knew. I would have loved to have a secret I could use to bribe Davey so he'd take me drowning out gophers the next time he went.

But it would still make a pretty good story, and I really was there when it happened. Fact is, I probably saved her life. For several days when Grandma, Papa and I had a cuppa Papa poured my tea into a saucer, added lots of sugar, blew it cool and as he put it in front of me, there was always a wink.

Joan and Betty with washing machine just like Grandma's
Summerland BC 2017

The Sandstorm

Hot that summer, it was, always suffocating with heat. Looking across Mike Kuczma's pasture past a dried up slough to the hills, even in early morning there were wavy lines in the sky. Not really lines I guess, but ripples of heat that made the sky above the hills look like water on a windy day. The day was going to be hot, hot, hot. As I sat on the steps of the back porch I shaded my eyes from the sun and scanned the sky like I'd seen my dad and papa do a lot that summer.

Daddy said if it didn't rain soon, there'd be no crops again, and more farmers would pack up and leave these parts. He sold Massey Harris farm machinery and nobody needed to buy that if there were no crops to harvest. Daddy said most folks couldn't afford to even put seeds in the ground 'cause they'd just shrivel up and blow away in the wind.

Worse than that, he said, he had to go collect payments on the threshing machine he'd sold to Jack Higgins last year. Jack was not a successful farmer, even when there was good weather, so he was pretty bad off most of the time. He was my daddy's cousin and had come out to Canada a few years before in hopes of making a good living for his wife, Rose, and their kids. But he'd never farmed before and Daddy said he just didn't have the knack. Because he was related, Daddy helped him buy the threshing machine on credit and helped him with seeding and harvest.

Dad spent a lot of time traveling around his territory visiting farmers, I think he knew everybody for miles around. He was big and friendly and had a laugh you could hear all over town. You pretty well knew where Cliff Thomas was, just by his laugh. He always seemed in a good mood when he was home and had lots of stories to tell us when he came back from his trips. Mama said he could see the funny side of just about anything.

And I knew that was true, because some of his best stories were about funerals and stuff. He loved to tell about going out one spring with the Consort undertaker to help him dig old man Thompson out of the grain in the granary where his sons had put him after he died. The winter was so bad they couldn't get to town and couldn't dig a grave, so they kept him frozen in the granary 'til they could give him a decent burial.

Daddy would always tell these stories with a half-smile on his face so his stories didn't seem scary to Davey and me. We'd listen, wide eyed. Mom, however, clicked her tongue disapprovingly. Grandma looked at him with disgust, "Oh, Clifford, you'll give these kids nightmares for sure." He didn't seem to take my grandma too seriously, just laughed and waved her off with his big ham hand.

Anyway, this day he was home. He and Papa were getting ready to go out to Jack Higgins' place. He was telling Papa how bad he felt. He didn't want to, but his boss told him that unless Jack had payment, he had to take back the thresher. Now my dad was big, and he could be tough, but when it came to helping people, he had a heart as big as could be, and this was a job he just couldn't bear to think about.

I followed Papa and Dad to the car. (Daddy had one of the only cars in town because of his job.) Much to my surprise, Daddy said, "Go tell your mom you're going with us, we should be back by lunch." It wasn't often I got a chance to go with Daddy, so I ran like the wind. Breathlessly I announced to the screen door that I was going, hoping Mom was in the kitchen and could hear. Then, afraid Davey had heard me and wanted to go, I turned and ran to the car. This was MY trip, I didn't want to share!

Dad got behind the steering wheel. I was happily seated between Daddy and Papa, feeling like I had the world by the tail. I didn't even care that Daddy's window was open and that smoke from Papa's cigarette brought tears to my eyes as it drifted by on its way to the window. No sir, I didn't care, and I sure wasn't going to cough if I could help it. I was with the men and I wasn't about to spoil that.

The road was dusty and rutted and the grass along the shallow ditches was as brown as the dirt. Barbed wire fences lined wide pastureland along the roadway. Here and there horses and cattle pawed hopefully at the ground trying to uncover a few blades of grass, raising small clouds of dirt with the effort. The sun, halfway to its high noon spot had taken on a faint hazy blur and no longer blazed down mercilessly. To the west, the sky had turned a sandy shade and the day was no longer bright but more like someone had pulled a curtain across that part of it.

Daddy said, "Looks like we could be in for a storm if the wind whips up."

Papa nodded, "Yep, no time to visit with Jack and Rose. Better just do your business. Wouldn't mind a beer in this heat, or at least a cuppa. Knowing Rose there won't be beer around. Poor old Jack doesn't have money for that."

We pulled into the farmyard. The few hens cackled off to their lean-to roost. A skinny dog put his tail between his legs and dived under the rickety porch that hung loosely from the front of the house. The house was small and weathered. A few shaky sheds lined the fence between the house and a barn that had seen better days. The barn, however, like those on most farms, had at least seen a coat of paint at some time. Faded red chips clung here and there. A huge hill of dried manure lurked behind it.

Jack opened the squeaking screen door, waved his hand at a crowd of flies waiting for a chance to get into the kitchen, called the dog from under the porch, and sauntered towards the car.

"Guess 'e ain't seen too many cars lately Cliff, or 'e'd of been a touch more friendly!" Jack's smile seemed a little pinched. He rolled a piece of straw back and forth between his teeth as he talked. He knew what

Daddy was there for, and was not going to make him say the words. He was too much of a gentleman for that. He reached through the open window and patted my head. "'ow's Joanie? You being a good girl? Don't know what you're 'anging around with these two fellas for. It's a sure thing they're up to no good." He winked.

Then not wanting to put off the bad news any longer, he waved toward a hill of sand banked up against the barn. Parts of a machine stuck out here and there but the constant wind and blowing soil had pretty well covered what was once a bright red Massey Harris threshing machine. "Guess you're gonna 'afta take it back, Cliff. It's a bloody cinch I can't pay anymore and there's no seed in the ground this year anyhow. Don't know what we're gonna do, but I guess it won't be farmin' much longer. 'Preciate your 'elp, don't blame you. You got a job to do. I know you wouldn't do it if you didn't 'ave to. There she is."

Dad stepped out of the car, put his arm around Jack's shoulders and they walked off a way. In a few minutes Daddy's familiar loud laugh boomed across the yard. He put his hand in his pocket and handed something to Jack, slapped him on the back, waved at the faces peering from behind the screen door and came back to the car. He got in, started the motor and we drove away.

No one said anything for a few minutes. My dad's eyes looked kind of funny. Finally he said, "You know, it's a funny thing, but I'll be Goddamned if I could find that machine. I guess I'll just have to wait and see if it turns up."

Papa grinned, rolled his cigarette across his lip and said, "By God Cliff, you're a damn fool."

The sky suddenly became important again. Wind whipped up little whirly funnels of dirt along the road. Russian thistles rolled recklessly across barren fields tumbling one after another into the fence, becoming trapped on barbed wire until another gust sent them scurrying and bouncing across the roadway in front of us. Now the wind was howling. Dirt and stinging sand ripped across ditches into our car windows.

Quickly Daddy rolled up his window, but not before our eyes and mouths felt gritty and stung with the force of the sand. Now the world outside was dark, not black, but a dirty whirling brown dark. The sound of sand hitting windows and the howl of the wind was everywhere. And worse, the road was nothing but a wide expanse of blowing soil. Ditches and fences were nowhere to be seen, Daddy fought with the steering wheel, not knowing where the road was.

All at once the car lurched as we hit the ditch careening into what had to be a fence. By this time, the sound of the storm was deafening and I was screaming at the top of my lungs. No longer was I thrilled to be there with the men, I just wanted to be home. My tears mixed with dirt and I felt grimy muddy stuff running down my cheeks into my mouth. My eyes stung and I could barely see the dashboard.

Daddy yanked the wheel and the car powered back up the rise and down the other side. A scraping noise on Papa's side of the car meant we had crossed the road and hit a fence again. *I knew we were going to die. I'd never see Mama or Davey or Grandma again.*

And whatever had happened to my daddy? He cursed, twisting the wheel back and forth, not even caring how scared I was. Papa hung on to the door handle. We bounced up, down and sideways while the car swerved back and forth each time we hit a fence. The heat was suffocating, it was hard to breathe. Sweat ran down my daddy's face like rain. I'd never seen him look so scary.

I don't know how long the storm lasted, but as quickly as it came, the wind died down and the horrid darkness began to clear. We were still moving and Daddy's eyes squinted as he tried to see through the sweat and dirt. Then he laughed. In front of us, as if by magic, the roadway appeared. "Jesus Christ, that was quite a ride! Thank God for the fences. We'll be home in no time. Quit your bawlin' and wipe your nose. You carry on like that and your mama will think we tried to kill you."

In all the excitement Papa had lost his cigarette and was frantically patting the front of his woolen trousers where a small hole was smouldering next to his zipper. "By God Cliff, your mother wouldn't forgive you if that 'ad caught fire!" He was chuckling and so was Daddy.

I didn't know what was so funny. I sniffled all the way back to town. That is, until it dawned on me, I had a story to tell Davey, one that he'd never believe!

Papa and Grandma Dunc Leave on the Train

I was four years old, I remember, standing on the railway station platform in Altario. Our whole family was there, Dad, Mama, Davey and Grandma and Papa Thomas. We were there to say goodbye to my other grandparents, Grandma and Papa Dunc. Dunc wasn't their last name, of course, it was McLeod. Papa's was Duncan and Grandma was Mame but for some reason we had always called them Papa and Grandma Dunc. Grandma was gentle and quiet and never seemed to mind.

But I knew that if we had tried that on Grandma Thomas there would have been trouble. She was too strong a person (I heard people say she wore the pants in the family) to put up with being called Grandma Dave.

So, there we were, hugged, kissed and hugged again. You see, they weren't just going on a trip. They were leaving on a long journey north to Fort Assiniboine, Alberta. Everything they owned was packed in boxcars.

The way Daddy explained it, farms couldn't grow crops anymore. There hadn't been rain since, "God only knows when, and all the good dirt had just up and blew away." So the government said people could have land up north to try again, and that's where my grandparents were going. Daddy and Papa talked a lot about how bad it was. If the farmers couldn't make it, "How the hell was anyone else supposed to live, and how come it took so damn long for the government to figure out we were in a depression?"

To a four year old this was confusing. All Davey and I knew was that people we loved were going away and everyone was really sad. Mama's youngest sister, Aunty Ruby, had already left for a job in Edmonton and Mama's other sister Aunt Meatie and her husband Uncle Maurice had gone north some time ago. Suddenly it seemed like we hardly had any family at all. I cried as the train pulled away from the station, especially when I saw Aunty Ruby's black saddle horse Mabel peering at me through the boards of a cattle car.

Yes, it was an unhappy day, that day in 1936. We stood and waved until the train got tiny. All that was left was a wiggly trail of black smoke where the engine had been. Daddy put his arm around Mama's shoulders and his eyes looked wet. Mama held our hands and squeezed so hard it made me blink. Then we all turned away and headed back down the street to Grandma and Papa's house for a cuppa. Papa said a beer would be a damn sight better but he just couldn't spare the dime.

For a long time things felt strange. I missed driving to the farm for Sunday dinner. It was pretty well always chicken with lots of potatoes and gravy and big slices of pie. Grandma Dunc said that pie was thanks to the government as dried apples came with relief shipments for prairie folk. I could see where the government was pretty important, even though I really had no idea what it was. I never really liked the dried fish they sent in wooden crates. But when my mama made white gravy to go with it, then it wasn't so bad.

Papa and Grandma Dunc

Life was different after Grandma and Papa left, but we looked forward to their letters. Life was hard, they were starting out on homesteads again. To own their land, my grandparents had to clear forest for farmland and build a home. Until they cut down and logged trees and removed stumps, there were no crops so they had to rely on garden crops and hunting deer and moose.

Fort Assiniboine

Papa and Grandma Dunc had been up north for a year when we visited them. Their closest town was a settlement called Fort Assiniboine. To reach it we had to cross the Athabasca River on a crude ferry that held two vehicles at a time. Crossing was slow. The ferry was attached to overhead cables to keep it from being taken downstream with the strong current. The ferry operator cast off from the dock, then with engine laboring to keep us going across the river and against the current, we slowly made our way to the other side. It was all very exciting for Davey and me, an adventure we had never experienced.

From that first trip on, every summer we spent time at "The Fort." Daddy took us and went on to visit machinery dealers in his "block," his sales territory. A few weeks later he picked us up for the trip home.

Davey and I loved the freedom of the farm, and spent most of our time at Aunt Meatie's. She and Uncle Maurice had a son Merle and daughter Jean who were close to our ages. Uncle Maurice was always in a good mood and let us tag along wherever he went and Aunt Meatie was a great cook. Although there were chores, it all seemed like fun to Davey and me.

There was always something to keep us busy. We spent time playing in the hayloft above the barn and once, on a dare, I jumped from the loft door to the ground below. It was quite a height and although I don't remember hurting myself, we all got into trouble and were forbidden to do it again.

Uncle Maurice had an old truck with the top cut off, and an open wooden box on the back. He called it "the Jitney," and drove it to town or to a neighbour's place. We would climb on the back and ride with him. No one ever fell off. It didn't go very fast so we probably wouldn't have hurt ourselves, except for a scrape or two. When it was time to go to Grandma and Papa Dunc's farm, a few miles away, Uncle Maurice drove the Jitney and Merle and Jean would come to stay there too.

Papa Dunc's milk cows wore bells around their necks because the trees in their pasture were so thick that it was hard to find them. At milking time Papa listened for the bells and we followed him to get the cows. Papa always cut a walking stick for himself and one for each of us. When we got the cows to the barn, they went into their stalls and Papa tied them for milking. It was fun to watch him milk the cows. Sometimes he said, "Open your mouth and I'll give you a drink." He'd turn the cow's udder upwards, and squeeze until the milk shot in a stream towards my mouth. It was very warm and sweet. *If I think hard I can still bring back the smell and taste of that milk.*

Although life was hard for my relatives, it was more of a lark for Davey and me. We were oblivious to hardship.

It was even an adventure to be chased out of Grandma's garden when caught invading her precious pea patch. Grandma Dunc had a passion for her peas. Even as we shelled them we were allowed to eat only a few. Grandma canned dozens of jars of peas each year for winter eating. (Sadly, when she passed away years later, her cellar was jammed with hundreds of jars of canned peas from years of preserving and apparently not so many winters of eating!)

Berry picking was fun but, for me, it was more the eating than the picking. Grandma always promised us a big strawberry shortcake with loads of real whipped cream and her shortcake biscuits were to die for!

Uncle Vic, Papa's brother, had a homestead not far away. He had the cleanest log house I had ever seen. No dirt floors for Uncle Vic, his were wood and were scrubbed clean. He was a bachelor and very fussy housekeeper so we kids were always nervous in case we spilled or tracked in something. He was always clean shaven and I still remember his shiny cheeks. Everything about him was just clean.

Our visits were full of things to do, hiking through bush, hide and seek and scaring each other with bear stories. There were bears but, in all my years there, I never saw one. One thing we did have to do, though, while dining on deer or moose meat, was to keep an eye on the main road. Most hunting was done illegally so the game warden was an unwelcome visitor. I never really liked wild meat, though. I usually filled up on new potatoes and carrots from Grandma's huge garden… and sometimes even peas.

When Daddy came to get us there were always tears. My Aunt Meatie was particularly emotional and Dad would try to hustle us into the car before she broke down during the goodbyes. One time the best thing happened. Crossing the river toward home our car broke down so we got to go back for a few days while parts came from Edmonton. Of course Dad wasn't happy, but as I mentioned, we were oblivious. A few days later we had to do the goodbye thing all over again.

Grandma and Papa Dunc, Aunt Meatie and Uncle Jack

Over the years there were many changes at Fort Assiniboine. The houses, once rustic log cabins, became new houses with cellars, wooden floors and homemade rugs to keep your feet toasty. My aunt and uncle built a big three bedroom house. At Grandma Dunc's house there always seemed to be room for everyone when we got together. Real walls replaced the sheets that used to be strung on lines to separate rooms. I remember a piano and when we were there Mama or Aunty Ruby played. We gathered around the piano and sang songs everyone knew.

I think there must have been a few bottles of beer to go round, everyone got really happy.

23

The Travelling Clinic, 1938

Davey and I were born in the nearest hospital, across the border in Loverna, Saskatchewan. The Altario hospital had long since been abandoned to pigeons. Still the largest building in town, it sat stark and remote in the field across the road from our house. The windows had disappeared and any paint that had covered its weathered siding had washed away with the years.

Rumors were rampant about things that happened there in its heyday but my only memory of it was that Aunt Ruby was born there. Most births took place at home with help of a neighboring midwife. As a small child, I often heard people talking about birth, death, illness and tragedy. Though being seen and not heard was expected, my brother and I were often privy to things we didn't really understand about the adult world.

People in the area relied on horseback or horse and buggy usually and automobiles were fairly rare. For longer trips, the train came through on weekdays, alternating directions every other day. Because the nearest hospital was quite far away, we were visited by the wonderful Travelling Clinic.

I was six years old when the school and town were abuzz with news that a clinic was coming and would be set up in the community hall for two days. The hall became a hive of activity as the day neared. Locals brought cots, sheets, chairs, tables, lamps and set them up neatly. We were to be visited by doctors and nurses who would arrive in large trucks, bringing with them many items needed to conduct examinations and minor surgeries.

Of particular interest to Davey and me was a large pit several men were digging behind the hall. We speculated that if anyone died that's where they would be thrown. A little harsh perhaps, but this was our first experience with such a momentous event. We were eager to believe even the goriest of explanations. Strangely enough, we were not so far wrong as you might think. We discovered that though the pit would not be the resting place of any unfortunate patients, it would become a resting place for any small body parts that were removed. Even this was enough excitement to keep the school kids buzzing, even though Mama said it was nothing for us to worry about. We watched closely for anyone in town who limped, coughed, or looked ill as a possible candidate for the pit.

Dad and Mom told us everyone was coming to the hall to be examined. Our eyes, ears, and throats were to be checked and if anyone had a problem it would be looked after. Only things like tonsils, adenoids, boils, sties, ingrown toenails, corns or ear wax and the like would be attended to, anything serious would be sent to Consort hospital. Consort, thirty-five miles away, was not an easy trip.

Well, the big day finally arrived. In the early morning two large covered trucks and a sort of bus lumbered up the road and came to a stop in front of the community hall. Davey and I woke early, the excitement was too much. We had gazed out the window since daybreak, watching for telltale dust to the southwest of town that would announce the arrival of the Traveling Clinic. We'd never seen trucks of this size before and could hear the growl of their motors long before they pulled into view.

Nearly everyone in town was on hand to greet the strangers. Men immediately started unloading cartons and carried them into the hall. School was closed for the day. The wide dusty main street was full of horse and wagon outfits, tractors pulling wagons, saddle horses hitched to rails and, here and there, a Model T looking quite out of place.

Shiny faced kids poured out of assorted wagons and buggies. Moms tried to keep them together in some sort of order and Dads hitched teams to available rails. Others drove off to Mike's livery barn where, for a fee, they could stable and feed their animals. It was going to be a busy time in our town. Except for Sports Day and the Christmas concert this was the biggest gathering I'd seen. Stores were already filling with kids dragging flustered mothers, begging to spend a penny on licorice pipes, candy hearts on strips of paper or packs of chiclets. There were lists of groceries to be filled through the day. Across the street at the hardware and lumber yard Mr. Atkins was starting to put together orders of supplies to be loaded in various wagons for the trip home. No sense making a trip to town on a perfectly good farming day unless you made it worth your while. It was going to be a warm one. No rain was a cause for a lot of griping and talk among the men. Most would spend a few hours at Ma Kuczma's hotel beer parlor at the end of the street before the day was over. Some would later rely on their horses knowing the way home without sober drivers.

Inside the hall, stage curtains had been pulled. It was being transformed into an operating room. On the main floor small cots were lined up along one side and down the middle. On the other side tables with lamps and chairs were arranged in little groups. The two doctors, in my six year old opinion, were very handsome. They busily unpacked strange, rather frightening looking tools from black bags and nurses carefully placed them in order on clean white cloths. *It's just like Grandma setting the table for Sunday dinner.* Each gleaming piece had its very own spot.

Now folks began to enter the hall slowly, not knowing what to expect. Mom took Davey and me firmly in hand as we took our place in line at one end of the room. To keep from getting bored, I amused myself by looking around the hall and making faces at my schoolmates. A sharp look from Mama stopped that, so I concentrated on what was going on ahead of us. The doctor asked one of the McCullough kids to stick out her tongue. I watched awestruck as the doctor shone a little flashlight inside her mouth. Suddenly I felt a hand smack me sharply and realized that I too had my tongue out. Our mom was usually gentle, but she hated for us to be rude.

The main tool, as far as I could see, was a flat wooden stick the doctor stuck in your mouth, followed by the command to say "ah." That seemed easy enough so when my turn came I happily obliged only to find myself gagging miserably. Then came the pointy ended light in my ears and up my nose. After this the doctor wrote on his notepad, then it was time for "a quick listen to the chest." He explained that the cold thing I felt between my shoulders was a stethoscope and asked me to breathe deeply.

Then he repeated the whole thing with my brother and made more notes. I giggled as Davey gurgled with the stick down his throat but when the doctor spoke quietly to my mother, glancing towards Davey and me, I stopped. Obviously, there was something terribly wrong with one of us. Maybe even both of us. My heart started to hammer as I thought of the pit outside, imagining all the things of mine that might end up there. *It wasn't fair, I was feeling pretty good and all of a sudden this wasn't so exciting after all. And Davey, sure, we'd had lots of fights, even hitting ones, but I really didn't want him to be sick! What if he had to go away to hospital? What if I had to?*

I remembered the day that Davey wouldn't let me go with him to hunt pigeons. I had actually chased him with a pair of scissors and would have thrown them, too, if Mama hadn't stopped me. I still remember the look on her face. She didn't spank or even yell. The quiet way she told me what a terrible thing I'd done made me cry more than any spanking.

Suddenly I just wanted to go home. The doctor turned his attention to the next one in line. Mama, Davey and I were free to go. Dad, helping to move beds, didn't even notice us. *Didn't he care that something awful was happening to his kids? My legs felt funny and my stomach hurt but I was too scared to ask Mama what the doctor had said.* We headed down the street. The hot dusty day and smell of horses wasn't exciting at all. I wanted to throw up.

Suddenly Mama smiled and told us how lucky we were. Davey's tonsils were going to come out and I was going to get rid of those nasty adenoids that made me have colds! Most kids, she said, had to get both done but the doctor said that's not necessary for you two. She laughed, "Isn't that wonderful?"

Davey and I looked at each other…wonderful? Maybe not, but if Mama could laugh about it, I guess we wouldn't die! Our mom then explained what would happen the next day. In the morning we would take our pajamas to the hall and would each have a bed. One at a time we would go up to the stage behind the curtain. We would be put to sleep, and when we awoke, it would all be over. No adenoids for me, no tonsils for Davey. A few hours later we could go home and have ice cream? That's it? No terrible disease, nothing to worry about, at least nothing big. Suddenly the day seemed good again, I felt like skipping. All I wanted to do was run and tell the other kids. I wondered who else would get to have an operation.

But first, I wanted to go over to see what was in that pit. I wasn't sure what tonsils looked like, or adenoids either. Seemed to me it was an awful big pit for stuff like that!

Making a Clean Breast of My Feelings

When I was five, Mama had to go away to hospital for an operation. Altario was close to the border and Macklin, Saskatchewan had the facilities and doctor to do the surgery.

Davey and I were too young to know at the time that the illness was cancer, breast cancer, and that the surgery was to completely remove Mama's left breast in hopes that the cancer would be cured. To make sure of this, she needed to travel to Edmonton for radiation treatments and, if the next five years went by without a return of the disease, they considered the cure totally successful.

All of this information was discussed in hushed whispers when our grandparents, uncles and aunts visited, so Davey and I heard bits and pieces. What we mainly heard was the word cancer, which struck terror to our hearts. Not long before, a young boy in town had died and people said it was from cancer. Another bit of talk mentioned that sometimes there was no pain until it was too late, people weren't to ignore strange lumps or sores. This, for a five year old and eight year old, was scary information. Davey and I were afraid to talk about it anymore.

However, I do remember immediately becoming wracked with worry. Alone in my bedroom, I began a daily study of my body. I was sure lumps were growing all over me, but I couldn't talk about it to anyone for what seemed like a long time.

One day Mama called me to her room as she was getting dressed and said that she thought I should see what the doctors had done. She bared her chest showing me the scars on her left side where a breast had once been and told me not to be afraid. Somehow she knew what my childish mind was going through. All my worries tumbled out as I showed her what made me afraid. She chuckled as she held me, reassuring me that all was well. The bumps I was afraid of were simply little muscles and ribs that everyone had.

I could hardly wait to tell Davey. My big brother scoffed at my worries, but I'm pretty sure he was relieved too. He just didn't want to talk about it.

From time to time that year, Mama had to go to Edmonton. She and Daddy went to the University Hospital for her radiation treatments.

Davey and I liked it when our Uncle Jack came to stay with us. He was my mom's fun younger brother and I guess he spoiled us a little so we wouldn't feel lonely. We didn't like to have our mama go away but she said it was important to make her all better, so it was worth it.

That winter an epidemic of whooping cough closed the school and Davey got to stay home. During this time Uncle Jack was looking after us while Mama and Daddy were in Edmonton. That's when Davey and I got whooping cough, both at the same time! All of a sudden our funny Uncle Jack was not having a good time. When we began to cough and throw up a lot he put Mama's wash tub in the middle of the kitchen floor for us. Poor Uncle Jack had a very weak stomach so every time Davey or I vomited, so did he. It wasn't fun being sick but it was kind of funny to watch Uncle Jack. It made him swear a lot. Was he ever glad when that was over with and our parents came home again!

That winter was one I will always remember.

The New School "Marm"

Late August days on the prairies were hot, dry and windy and that day was typical. Despite the weather, there was an air of excitement in Altario. My little town was expecting a new teacher and today was the day she was due to arrive. We knew it was a she because very few men took to the teaching profession, the pay just wasn't enough.

The last teacher was also a lady. She had moved on to bigger and better things and to a wider choice of male companionship after a short and unrewarding relationship with one Jack McLeod, who happened to be my uncle.

The one room school stood proudly on a small rise on the west side of town. Today it sported a brand new coat of pale yellow paint. Just a short distance away the two room teacherage with matching paint waited clean and shiny to welcome its new occupant. The teacher was a most respected person in town, so no expense or labor was spared to make her stay pleasant and comfortable. After all, not everyone with a teaching certificate wanted to come to an out-of-the-way spot like ours to pursue a career. The fact that this was her first job and that her choices were therefore limited probably determined our new school marm's placement here.

Local folks were anxious to put on a good showing, everyone was dressed for the occasion. Mike, owner of the livery barn, strolled in a brand new pair of blue overalls and a crisp white shirt, his friendly moon-shaped face shiny and freshly shaven. He knew his livery would have customers because farmers would come to greet the newcomer. Many would use his barn to feed and water their teams.

Better yet, there was no doubt that the local hotel and beer parlor owned and ably run by his wife, Mary (better known as Ma K.), would be a popular spot for men to gather. Yes, I said men. The sign on the entrance read, "Licensed Premises, Ladies and Escorts" which according to liquor laws meant only men could enter alone. Females, on the other hand, had to be accompanied by a man if they wished to enjoy a glass of foamy brew. Legal or not, any self-respecting woman risked sullying her reputation if seen entering the beer parlor. If anyone in town was likely to keep a watchful eye, it was Grandma Thomas. Her kitchen table at the south end of Main Street afforded a perfect view of pretty well everything all the way up the street.

Since it was a weekday, Cohoe's Grocery and Atkin's Hardware would do well. The only mechanic in town, Joe Kreiser, would probably have machinery parts to repair.

Prominent among waiting residents were the area's eligible bachelors, a total of two. One was Uncle Jack, who ran one of the grain elevators that stood along the railway track. The other, a farmer and only son of a large family, Gordon, was well known to everyone. He had a child-like innocence that made him a bit of a character. Taken less seriously than his age and size demanded, he was big, good natured and eager to please, but often the butt of jokes he did not understand. Uncle Jack, on the other hand, was a smoothie with a reputation for being a pretty good guy. He was a bit on the wild side, reasonably good looking and, most importantly, drove one of few cars around. He was athletic and, from my point of view, a lot of fun. It was no secret that young single women were rare here, and as a result ardently sought after. Gordon and Jack certainly wanted to be among the first to look over the new arrival.

I had just had a very big day of my own the week before, celebrating my sixth birthday, so my interest in the new teacher was personal. I was about to start school so that made today an even bigger event for me. Up to now I had only heard tidbits about what went on at school. Davey did his best to keep me in awe of his three years of experience.

My best pal was the son of a Ukrainian family. Luckily, he was also starting school so I would not be alone in the "grade one row," as

Davey described it. Stanley and I were pretty well inseparable outside but, for reasons I didn't understand, I was seldom allowed in his house. Also, he seemed to hang back when invited into ours. When I called on him to play, his little sister Rosie answered the door, called to her mother using words I didn't understand, and closed the door. I waited on the step, not sure if Stanley would come out or not. In winter I was invited inside and offered a chair. His mother nodded and went about her work in the kitchen. There was always a delicious aroma rising from kettles on her stove and I secretly wished my mom would make whatever Stanley's mom was constantly cooking. Conversations at his house were strange to me but, with nothing to do but listen while waiting, some words began to have meaning. I often repeated them to myself or just made up meaningless words. This became such fun that I spent hours chattering meaningless garble with only the two dogs, Brownie and Jerry for listeners. They jumped up, barked and ran around, doing their best to follow what seemed to be instructions. Except for Stanley, they were my closest buddies. They were really Grandma and Papa Thomas's dogs, but I thought of them as my own and hoped they wouldn't forget me when I started school.

The daily train was due to arrive at noon. Davey and I were with Papa while he busied himself getting mailbags ready to send out. We were sort of hoping he'd remember he hadn't given us a penny yet today and, though he rarely forgot, it seemed like a good idea to try to be helpful just in case. Today he was in a hurry and we were in the way. Papa never minced words. As I stumbled over a mailbag, he let out a string of expletives that sent me flying out the door. We'd learned not to take Papa's swear words too seriously but sometimes he meant it more than others. This was one of those times so we decided to take our chances with pennies and left quietly. We would tag along when Papa started out with the mail.

The station was busy when the train came and though we had a lot of freedom to roam, that was one time when we had to stay close to Papa, or else!

There were more bags than usual today, end of the month stuff, Papa said, so instead of tossing them over his shoulder, he took the heavy wagon he had built for this job. Those mailbags were awfully big and Papa was a little man, but somehow he heaved them around. When Daddy was home he insisted on carrying them, much to Papa's disgust.

Anyway, finally it was time to go to the station. Davey and I followed behind as Papa pulled the rumbling wagon down the dusty street. A lot of people were heading for the station and a distant sound of a whistle drifted across rolling hills to the west. As a wisp of smoke appeared on the horizon we knew the train was minutes away. In the excitement I started to run and Papa tugged harder at the tongue of the wagon. No one wanted to be late today.

The station platform was crowded. I spotted Uncle Jack looking pretty handsome in a clean shirt, opened at the neck so you could see a hint of the curly hair on his chest. Uncle Jack had curly hair on his head too but there was a round bare spot on top so I guess it made him feel good to show he still had hair in other places. I was proud that he was my uncle. Davey and I tried hard to stay on his good side. He was fun and knew what kids like to do but, if he caught us doing something wrong, he was quick to smack us and send us packing. That had happened on more occasions than we liked to admit so we were always on guard. Today he had other things on his mind so all we got was a quick wave.

Daddy was helping someone fix a tractor. Mom, Grandma and other ladies were setting up a nice lunch at the community hall to welcome the teacher. There were tarts, cakes and little sandwiches. Mom had made sandwiches with cheese and pickle filling and had trimmed off the crusts. Davey and I watched carefully, eating most of the trimmings, leaving only those that lacked filling. We'd had our orders, we would not be guests at the community hall lunch!

Finally the train pulled into the station. As usual, the engineer leaned out his cab window waving. It was a short train today, only one passenger car, a stock car and a couple of boxcars separated the huge puffing engine from the caboose at the rear. Harvesting was not fully underway, so no need for grain cars yet.

The conductor, dressed in his navy uniform and peaked cap, swung precariously from the step on the caboose signalling to the engineer that it was okay to stop. I was always fascinated by the way he hung by one arm to the handrail and one foot on the step, leaning out as far as possible so the engineer could get a clear view of him. With a grinding squeal, the train rolled to a full stop releasing a final hiss of steam.

All eyes were fixed on the passenger car as the conductor rushed ahead to pull the steps into place. Mr. Atkins, chairman of our school board, and official greeter, stepped forward, adjusting his tie. Everyone waited expectantly. A muffled groan was heard as the first passenger to alight turned out to be Albert Murphy, home after a short stay in Consort Hospital. He'd fallen off his barn roof and for his efforts wore a splint on one leg and a sling on his arm. After good natured greetings someone yelled, "What's the other guy look like?"

Yes, Uncle Jack McLeod did marry my Grade One teacher Miss Reinnikka. She was also my Grade Three teacher Mrs. McLeod! Aunt Alla taught for many years in Cochrane Alberta.

But another person appeared at the top of the step. It was suddenly quiet. I will always remember the slim figure, dressed in a blue and white knitted suit and high heels like I had never seen before. She wore a matching hat, perched at a jaunty angle, and beneath it tumbled brown wavy hair. She smiled and I sighed. *She is the most beautiful person I've ever seen.*

Mr. Atkins took her hand as she stepped from the train. He introduced himself, then turned to address the crowd. "Folks, meet Miss Alla Reinnikka, your new school marm." I honestly don't remember if he really said "marm." Mr. Atkins was always very proper in his talk but that's what everyone else called her, and that was good enough for me.

Uncle Jack was pretty fast on his feet, probably because he was a good ball player. He reached her just in time to take two heavy suitcases the conductor unloaded from the passenger car behind her. He had a grin on his face as wide as anything. The shiny gold filling in his side tooth glittered in the sun as he introduced himself.

Right then and there, something seemed to be happening that I didn't understand but I was pretty sure it was good.

By this time, everyone was moving away towards town hall and Papa was loading the new mail on his cart. Davey and I left with him.

"Isn't she beautiful, Davey? Have you ever seen anyone that pretty?" Davey, being a boy, wasn't likely to get that excited, but I could tell he was pretty impressed.

School was going to be wonderful, I thought.

Templeton's Hill

Finally we were there, at the top of the hill. It had been a long, hard, hot job but, as we all stood at the top looking down over the rock strewn hillside that sloped toward town, we heaved sighs of relief. One by one we sank to the ground. Our bare arms and legs glistened with sweat. Noisy black flies buzzed around us. It was supposed to rain, Papa said that morning, and flies were always bad just before a rain.

It was hard to believe we had really done it. There, at the very top of the hill, was Mike Kuczma's dray wagon. It had been a struggle but somehow, with nearly every kid in town helping, we pushed, pulled and heaved the heavy dray all the way up the gently sloping east side of the hill.

It had been my cousin Keith's idea. He was really our mom's cousin, but he and his sister Marguerite were only a few years older than Davey. It was exciting when they came to town for a visit. Keith was tall for his age, with a laugh that was always just waiting for a chance. Marguerite had red hair and freckles and a terrible temper to match. She always had to be the boss. I probably wasn't supposed to be part of the group. I was a lot younger, but that morning when I heard Keith, Davey and Marguerite whispering, I made a fuss and said I'd tell, so they let me come. Pretty well all the kids in town were there, except Stanley's little sister Rosie who was too small to go anywhere. Helen and Jean Kuczma, their brother Alec, Johnny Templeton who lived in the only house on the hill, and the Aronyk kids, who lived in the section house across the tracks from the station were all there.

Not only was it a huge job hauling that wagon uphill but we had done it without being noticed by any of the adults in town! After all, I don't think there was a tree in town, except for the caraganas that lined the

37

roadside and a few low bushes that grew wild in the pasture behind our house. The houses and buildings were not close together so it was pretty hard to do anything sneaky without being caught. To take the town dray all the way from the livery barn, across Main Street, up the lane past Kreiser's garage and then on up the hill, without being noticed by anyone in town, was an accomplishment. On top of that, we had escaped the eagle eye of Grandma Thomas.

We rested for a while eating crackers and cheese from a jam pail Davey had packed, telling Mom we were going for a picnic. We took turns drinking from the pump behind Templeton's house. Now we were ready for the real fun. The hard work behind us, we pushed the wagon easily to the south crest of the hill. Looking down, my stomach felt funny and my skin got prickly. I looked at my arms and saw that the hairs were all standing straight up. I was no longer sweating and my mouth filled with saliva just like when you throw up. The hill on this side dropped sharply. There had been a road of sorts, but it was overgrown and rutted. Sharp rocks lay half hidden on the trail.

I wanted to run but it was too late, all the kids were piling on the flat, open bed of the dray. Keith and Alec lifted the wagon tongue off the ground, swinging it back over the wagon. Davey gave me a boost. I slid on my hands and knees into the middle as he climbed on beside me. There was nothing to hold except for a few boards at the very front. We all sat crowded in the centre holding on to each other.

Keith held the tongue while Alec gave the wagon a push, jumping on as it started to lurch over the crest of the hill. He and Keith wrapped their arms around the thick wooden wagon tongue and held on hard trying to steer the metal wheels into the ruts. The wagon picked up speed. We were hurtling down the steep slope, bouncing up and down as the wheels hit rock after rock, throwing Keith and Alec wildly from one side of the wagon to the other as they attempted to hold on and steer. Everyone screamed and rolled back and forth on the wagon bed, trying desperately to keep from being thrown over the side. My brother held on to me but we were bumping heads and scraping knees on the rough boards and it seemed it would never end. All the time we slid closer to the front of the dray, closer and closer to the wildly swinging tongue. Alec and Keith were flying back and forth with its momentum.

All at once the hard metal wheels hit a huge rock jutting out of the hill. The tongue swept across the wagon, Alec and Keith were flying with it. At the same time, the whole wagon lurched sideways on two wheels and we soared through the air, rolling and tumbling down through grass and weeds in a cloud of dust. There was a grinding crash as the dray roared down the last few feet of the hill and rolled over on its side. Its twisting axle and upturned wheels looked sort of like a dog waiting to have his belly scratched.

Most of us were crying. Everyone had cuts and bruises. Keith's nose was bleeding and he had a huge lump on the side of his head. Our clothes were torn and one of my shoes had even come off in my tumble downhill. I guess there must have been a lot of noise because our little venture was no longer a secret.

Keith and Alec helped the little kids up. Marguerite did a lot of yelling at Keith for not steering better. Mike Kuczma, generally a smiling happy man, jumped up and down, yelling in Ukrainian. Only his own kids knew what he was saying but no one dared move or say a word as he walked around the broken hulk that had been his dray.

We dragged ourselves home but not before news of our misadventure reached Mama. We were both very glad Daddy was travelling and wouldn't be home for a few days.

Of course, I was not held to blame, too young to know better, but I know Alec and his sisters spent the rest of the summer weeding, herding cattle and cleaning the livery barn. That is, when they weren't helping Ma Kuczma cook and clean at the hotel. Keith and Marguerite did go home the next day, though I'm pretty sure they suffered some kind of punishment. We didn't see Johnny for quite a while and Stanley couldn't come out to play for days. Davey spent most of his time at the Post Office with Papa helping with mailbags.

I'm pretty sure we didn't get our regular penny a day for quite a few days.

By the time Daddy came home things had settled down quite a bit. Mama told him the whole story. He gave us both a good scolding but there seemed to be just the hint of a smile and a twinkle in his eyes.

There was a new dray in town, though.

Being a Kid on the Prairies

There was a time when I'd sit down and words would start to flow,
then what I wrote was satisfying, interesting, you know.
I wrote about my childhood, as a kid out in the west,
living in a little town, and life just seemed the best.

Oh, it wasn't always perfect, or even close to that,
but we were a loving family with dogs and one white cat.
We sledded in the winter on a hill just out the back,
and slid on frozen ponds, while we dared the ice to crack.

The summers we went wading or rafting on the sloughs,
made slingshots and arrow guns with what we found to use.
We'd pack up cheese and crackers and head off to the hills,
in search of Indian burial grounds or other equal thrills.

Or maybe take the dog, a string and water pails,
and go out to drown gophers, a penny for their tails.
Looking back that seems so heartless, and I feel a little sad
but our skills in that department were really pretty bad.
(Our old dog got excited when they popped out of the ground,
and barked so hard they ran away before they ever drowned.)

We'd trek out to the graveyard, then try to scare each other,
moaning sounds behind tombstones was a favorite of my brother.
The summer days were easy, there was always lots to do.
No, we didn't go to movies or have trips to see a zoo.
There was pick up ball, kick the can, or sometimes hide and seek.
If you were IT you hid your eyes, counted to ten and didn't peek,
then tore off looking everywhere to find each hidden friend,
and if you couldn't find them all, then you'd be IT again!

But sometimes all your buddies, even the dogs and cat,
would tire of playing games, go home, and that was that!
But Mom was always waiting to listen to our story
and somehow our adventures were not a cause to worry.

Rubber Ice

There still wasn't snow that fall but it was cold. Mama had washed clothes the day before because it was a Monday. I guess that was washday pretty well all over town. The night before Daddy had to go out and bring in water from the rain barrel to fill the big copper boiler on the stove so it would be hot by morning. He had to break ice at the top of the barrel to get water and told Mama that if it didn't snow soon and the rain barrel froze, he would have to haul water from the slough. That meant chopping a big hole in the ice which wasn't easy to do because the ice kept cracking around the hole. I knew that from a story Papa loved to tell. Daddy once broke through and fell in the slough, and by the time he got home he could hardly move because his clothes froze stiff.

There was a town well but Daddy said, with all the dry weather, no one could use that water for anything but drinking.

I liked walking around town on washday. It was fun to see all the clothes hanging on lines, especially when they were frozen. Long white underwear looked like ghosts dancing a silly, stiff dance. From our house, looking up and across toward Atkin's house, Mr. Atkin's long johns and Mrs. Atkin's big blue bloomers moved side by side and seemed to be hanging at the top of the big black letters on the United Grain Growers elevator. *I wish Uncle Jack could see that, I bet he'd think of*

Davey and Joan

42

something funny to say. Uncle Jack always said something to make us laugh, although sometimes Mama frowned at him. She said if he had kids he wouldn't be so rude but she never really got upset.

So that day, Davey and I went off to school with Mom calling after us to be careful and to stay off the ice. You see, there was a little slough at the bottom of the hill where our school stood. It was easy to go around it but it was so tempting to see if we could wade through without water going over the top of our rubber boots. However, it had been freezing for a few days and, when Davey and I got there, kids were already daring each other to see who could run across the ice without falling through. One farm boy made it safely across with the ice bouncing up and down under his feet, just like rubber. Two or three kids followed him safely, the ice going up and down crazily, just like sheets when Grandma and Mama shook them out to hang on the line. Kids were yelling, "Who is going to be next?" Everyone was jumping up and down even if they weren't on the ice.

My heart was pounding with excitement. It was my first winter at school so this was new for me. I looked down at my new rubber boots and I just knew I would be next. Without looking at Davey, I headed for the slough at full speed, sliding wildly into the centre where water oozed up through weakened ice. My heart was in my throat and my face felt hot. Without a doubt I knew I wouldn't make it. Somewhere behind me I heard Davey yelling to come back but it was too late! Suddenly the ice opened up and down I went flopping helplessly in icy cold water. *I'm going to drown and everyone will be so mad at me.* I was sobbing and so cold when it came to me that I wasn't sinking anymore. I was sitting there on the bottom with water around my waist, just sitting in a hole in the ice. All the kids were laughing, that is, all but Davey. He was mad.

Suddenly the laughter died down. I heard Miss Reinnikka's voice. "Joan, get up and get out of there right now! You are in big trouble!"

Dripping and shivering, I slogged my way back to the shore, still in tears. Miss Reinnikka, however, was having none of it. There would be no sympathy. I was unceremoniously marched up the hill to the school by my teacher. Behind her came all the kids trying hard not to giggle in order to avoid Miss Reinnikka's wrath.

I spent the rest of the morning alone in a blanket, out in the dreaded hallway. My soaking clothes sizzled as they dried near the pot-bellied stove at the back of the class. My rubber boots stood bottoms up draining.

It was not a perfect day.

Passing Grade One

School was out! I ran home full of excitement waving my report card high in the air. I passed, I passed. *Next year I would be in Grade 2!* And to make it even more perfect, Miss Reinnekka gave us chocolate covered suckers bigger than any I'd ever seen.

Grades 1 to 3 got to go home early. The other kids still had tests to write. Somehow they needed more room and I didn't understand why. When I asked, Miss Reinnekka said it was to make sure no one could see anyone else's answers.

I would have five more days of summer holidays than my brother and could hardly wait to get started. I reached the post office where Papa was sorting mail. He was whistling through his teeth as always, and waved to me in the doorway. I showed him my report card and, just as I hoped, he reached into his pocket and took out a penny but stopped and pulled his hand back. My heart stopped, had I done something wrong? The eager hand I held out slowly dropped to my side, my report card forgotten.

As I have said, Papa gave me a penny every day unless I did something wrong. Like the time I knocked a whole can of turpentine on his floor and it smelled just awful for days and days. I didn't get a penny for a while then. But Davey did and it bothered me something terrible. Even Davey felt bad and shared his licorice pipes that were my absolute favorites.

But after a moment Papa laughed and ashes from his cigarette dropped all over the floor. "'Ere, 'ere, what's the long mug about? Don't you want this?"

I looked up, trying to keep my lip from shaking, and there, in the palm of his open hand, was a beautiful, big, shiny nickel. My world was right again, Papa was just teasing and I'd fallen for it. With the nickel burning

45

hotly in my hand, I ran home to tell Mama about Grade 2, getting out early and the nickel from Papa.

Slamming the screen door, I ran in breathlessly. Mama and Grandma sat at the table having a cup of tea. I couldn't decide which good news to tell first: that I had passed, or that Papa gave me a nickel. It didn't take Mama long to straighten me out there. Mama had been a teacher so school definitely came first. I fidgeted from one foot to the other while the two of them studied my report card. I was planning which candy I would get at the Red and White Store as soon as Mama let me go.

Finally Mama smiled and said, "Oh, alright, I know you want to spend your money. Papa sure does spoil you two. Go ahead but be sure you bring most of your candy home and leave that sucker with me. Your teeth will fall out for sure if you eat that all at once." I was gone, the screen door slamming behind me once again.

The Red and White Store was just a short walk, as was pretty well everything in town. Mr. and Mrs. Pearl ran the store with their sons. They were friendly and everyone in town called Mr. Pearl "Benny." He was a happy man with greying curly hair and he wore big gold rings on his pudgy hands. You noticed his hands because he never let us kids take candy out of the jars ourselves. We just pointed. Then he reached into the wide mouthed candy jars with a silver scoop and carefully counted the candies out loud, moving each piece aside with his finger so we could count with him. His fingernails were very clean and cut very short. He always wiped his hands on his apron before taking our money.

Daddy said if there was anybody honest in the whole town, it was Benny Pearl. The store was a wonderful place. There were groceries and cans on shelves and a big wooden barrel with a lid that was full of soda crackers. Next to that, at the end of the counter, sat a huge round wheel of yellow cheese with a knife stuck in the top. Mr. Pearl kept it covered with a clean cloth to keep flies away. People could come in, lean on the counter and nibble on a cracker and a piece of cheese. Only if they were good customers. Daddy said Benny Pearl is honest but you don't eat his crackers and cheese until you've bought something. Even then, you don't dip into that cracker barrel more than once or twice or Benny would be there like a flash and the lid would go down.

Daddy said folks who take advantage of a good thing soon wear out their welcome.

Summer Holidays

Summer holidays had started out good, there was so much to do I began to wonder if I really wanted to be in Grade 2.

Grandma and Papa's two dogs, three legged Brownie and Boston terrier Jerry, were my best friends. Grandma and Papa treated those dogs like their other kids. The dogs got to clean off plates after meals (our mom hated that) and even if they were in the way, no one made the dogs move. We stepped over them and sometimes tripped over them. I loved staying overnight 'cause the dogs could sleep on the bed with me. Davey wasn't so lucky because of his allergies and asthma. But the dogs were always happy to be with me and when Davey and I took our pails off to the edge of town to "drown out" gophers, they eagerly tagged along.

Grandma and Mama took me with them to Ladies Aid meetings. Grandma had learned to drive the black Model A Ford coupe Papa bought and, as far as I could tell, she was the only lady in town who knew how to drive. Mostly it was men who drove but Grandma wouldn't have any of that. If there was a car in the family, she was going to drive!

I got to sit in the middle and had to keep my knees out of the way so Grandma could reach the gear shift that stuck out of the floor. Papa had to turn the crank in front as Grandma stepped on the gas, then he'd jump out of the way as we lurched out of the yard with Grandma trying to remember clutch, gas pedal and gear shift all at once. We'd tear off in a cloud of dust. Papa yelled orders 'til we were out of sight.

It was a rough enough ride over ruts in the road but, with Grandma, changing gears never came easy. Though I thought the ride was great fun, it didn't seem like Mama enjoyed it very much. By the time we reached the farm where the ladies were meeting, Mama and Grandma had to take a few minutes to straighten their hats and brush off dust from the trip.

I played with whatever kids were lucky enough to be there with their moms. The best part of the whole day was the little sandwiches (with no crusts!) and cakes with mountain high icing. I loved Ladies Aid. For the trip home, Grandma had to ask the man of the house to turn the crank to start the car. I wasn't sure what we would do if the car stopped part way and needed to be cranked. But it never did happen on Ladies Aid day.

One day Mama said we were going to visit Mrs. Templeton. The Templetons were from Scotland and had two sons. The youngest, Johnny, was Davey's best friend. They lived on a hill just outside of town that you could see from our place. Their hill was covered with big rocks and was a great place to play. Sometimes Davey and I took shovels to the hill 'cause we heard that there was an Indian burial ground there. Mama said there was no such thing but she didn't see any harm if we wanted to see what we could dig up, which was nothing most of the time.

This day Mrs. Templeton was waiting for us with tea and scones. Then Mama told me the real reason for our visit. Mrs. Templeton was a seamstress and was going to make me a new dress. Now if there was one thing my mama and I didn't agree on, it was me and dresses! I was perfectly happy to wear just about anything but a dress! Mama said girls had to have a nice dress for Sunday school and special occasions and Mrs. Templeton was nice enough to offer to make one for me at very little cost.

I had no choice, I was getting a new dress. To my horror it was going to be bright pink in some shiny cloth with lots of ruffles. I stood teary-eyed in my underwear while Mrs. T measured and pinned the horrid pink stuff around me. Mama coaxed me to stand still.

The best part of that visit was the scones!

It took two more visits for "fittings" and Mama said I could go alone. The bad part of that was Mrs. Templeton wasn't nearly as nice when Mama wasn't there and she spoke sharply if I wiggled. I didn't understand her Scottish accent very well but there was no doubt what she meant.

Also when Mama didn't come there were no scones.

The Church

I really didn't understand why most people in town got to go to the big church with the steeple. I knew it was called the Catholic Church and every Sunday people from the country came to town, hitched their teams to the rail in front of the church, and went inside. The kids from the section house were Catholic so they went too.

I asked Mama how come we didn't have a building like that. Instead, Davey and I always went with Mama up to the Cohoe house for Sunday school.

Mrs. Cohoe was a big woman with salt and pepper hair pulled up tight behind her head like a bun. Her daughter lived with her. Everyone said they were "God-fearing people." They owned a grocery store across from the hotel and they did all the work there themselves.

Mama said, years ago they had a farm.

Mr. Cohoe was carrying milk pails to the house in a storm and was hit by a lightning bolt. Daddy said it was a pretty good way to get yourself killed. I decided that was a good thing to remember. Daddy said that the nature of Mr. Cohoe's death was common knowledge in town. I had noticed that when someone asked a dumb question, Daddy said, "Well, and did you know old Cohoe died?" Mama said sarcasm wasn't nice. But I heard many people say that same thing so I guess sarcasm wasn't as bad as Mama thought it was.

Anyway, Sunday mornings we went to the Cohoe's and Nina Cohoe (she wore her hair in a bun too and it made her look really cranky) sang hymns like "Jesus Loves Me" and "God Sees the Little Sparrow Fall." I really liked singing and it made me feel proud that our mama could play the piano. Mrs. Cohoe sometimes gave us cookies after church while she and Nina had tea with Mama. We liked that too.

It was usually a pretty nice time, even if Mama scolded us later for looking around or not bowing our heads for prayers. It was hard sometimes because Mrs. Cohoe could think of an awful lot of things to pray about. She must have thought we were pretty bad because she kept asking God to forgive our sins, over and over.

I hoped God couldn't always tell what I was thinking but, then again, if he saw every sparrow fall, he very likely knew all about me, too. It made my stomach hurt just thinking about it. I squeezed my eyes shut and tried really hard not to think of anything bad.

At the end I said "Amen" really loud to make sure everyone knew I was listening.

The Move

That summer it hardly ever rained so almost all days were hot and sunny. I played outside all the time and never had to wear dress-up clothes or get my hair braided so I guess I was the "Ragamuffin" that Grandma always called me.

It was on just that kind of day that I was running up the hill to Papa and Grandma's house. I stopped when I saw a stranger talking to Daddy. He wore a grey suit with a matching tie and a fedora. (Papa said that's what they were called. My daddy wore one travelling "on the road," but to Daddy it was just a hat. I liked the word "fedora" but it seemed to me it should be the name of a bright colored flower, not a dull grey hat.) Anyway, the man in the grey suit was very important looking. You could tell he wasn't like other men in town. He had a shiny new car and it was grey, too. I knew he must be special because there were hardly any cars in town. So when Daddy told me his name was Mr. Peterson and he was going to be Daddy's new boss, I wasn't surprised. He sort of looked like a boss. Daddy was quitting his travelling job to work for United Grain Growers as an elevator operator. That seemed funny to me, I knew there already was a United Grain Growers operator in Altario. Mr. Peterson smiled, trying hard to be friendly but when he talked to me it was like the way Davey talked when he wanted my tapioca pudding after he'd already eaten his, trying to convince me it was a good idea.

We had lived in Altario all my life. At seven that seemed like a long time and now this man wanted us to move to Provost, a big town nearly forty miles away!

Daddy and Mama had taken us there once to a movie show *Snow White*. I remembered how scared I was because it had rained all day and the road was so muddy and slippery. I'd never been in a movie theatre before.

Once I watched a silent movie at our community hall, where someone played the piano fast or slow or loud or soft. I guess that helped you to know when to be scared or excited if you couldn't tell from the pictures. It was kind of fun but, just when it got interesting, a man stopped the picture to put on a new roll of film.

Snow White was different. The people on the screen talked and there was music and when Snow White sang I wanted to be just like her. I covered my eyes and hid in Mama's coat when the Wicked Queen appeared in the mirror.

We moved that summer and I had to say goodbye to Papa and Grandma and their dogs. Grandma and Mama both cried until Papa said, "Oh, give over, it's not the end of the world." But he did take the cigarette out of his mouth to give us all a hug and a kiss. His sweater smelled like wood shavings and smoke while Grandma always smelled like talcum powder. *I knew I would really miss those smells.*

Provost was an adventure, from the beginning it was like a different world. When I stood in the middle of the street near the town pump in Altario I saw almost every house in town. Provost was so big that, when we drove in, we saw only the elevators and the nearest streets. There were sidewalks everywhere, not just in front of stores, and trees in every yard! Our house had a fence with a caragana hedge around it. Our new house was small, but there was one more bedroom so Davey and I didn't have to share. There wasn't an upstairs or basement, just a door in the floor and a ladder. I wouldn't go down there, it was dark and smelled like wet laundry. There was a wooden sidewalk from our kitchen door to a garage and outhouse and behind that was a back alley. One thing in the kitchen was different. Instead of a pail of fresh water with a dipper sitting beside the sink, there was a pump that came right out of the countertop, just like the one in the street in Altario, but a lot smaller.

"A nice modern touch," Mama said.

Soon we got to know the neighbours. They had a girl Davey's age named Alicia and she had a big cat she named "Bum." It was fun to stand in the yard yelling, "Here Bum, where are you Bum?" or, better still, when Alicia came over, "Did you bring your Bum with you?" But that didn't go over very good with Mama.

Alicia, who had lived in Provost all her life, decided to show Davey and me the ways of life in her big town. Davey soon tired of Alicia's opinions on how to behave and who to make friends with, and drifted off to find his own buddies. I, however, was thrilled that someone so grown up and smart would let me tag along. I hung on her every word, although she made it clear that once school started, she would be in Grade 5 and, since I would only be in Grade 2, I couldn't expect to hang around with her or her friends. Undaunted, I was happy to take any time she kindly gave me. I wished summer could last forever.

One of our first adventures was a walk downtown. Alicia proudly showed me the movie theatre and said, "Every Saturday afternoon there's a matinee, kids go for ten cents." This sounded wonderful, except I wasn't really sure what "matinee" was. I thought I'd wait and ask my mama so Alicia wouldn't think I was dumb.

When I got home, I asked Mama if I could go to a Saturday matinee with Alicia. Mama said it would be fine since it was an afternoon show. There, my question was answered, a matinee was an afternoon movie! Alicia said I could go with her and her friends but, if there weren't enough seats together, I might not be able to sit with them. This was okay with me, I was used to spending time alone. Davey didn't always like me hanging around and in Altario there had been hardly any kids my age.

When Saturday came, Mama carefully counted out two nickels, smiled, and put another five pennies in my hand. "You might want to buy a treat at the theatre," she said.

I was thrilled. At the theatre I was secretly happy to find I couldn't sit with Alicia and her friends. I wouldn't have to share my popcorn. The movie was about cowboys and Indians. There were lots of horses, gunfights and noise and the faster the horses galloped and the louder the Indians whooped, the faster I shoved popcorn in my mouth. Before I knew it, the bag was empty and my stomach didn't feel too good. When the movie ended, I left the kids and ran home as fast as I could. At home, I headed straight for the kitchen sink. There I threw up all my popcorn, this right in front of Mama and a neighbour lady who had dropped in to welcome us to town. Mama said later it sort of spoiled their appetites for tea and scones.

From then on popcorn didn't hold the same attraction for me. Saturdays I spent my extra pennies on bubble gum or candy.

Summer holidays went by quickly, every day was new and exciting. There was a fair in town. My daddy and Uncle Jack (who drove up from Altario) threw darts at balloons and baseballs at milk bottles trying to win the big prizes behind the counter for us. We didn't ever get the big ones though. The bottles didn't fall over that easily even when Uncle Jack hit them with a ball and the balloons wobbled and rolled so hardly any darts popped them. The man behind the counter kept calling out to people to come over and try their luck. Finally Daddy and Uncle Jack stopped paying for tries and the man gave Davey and me suckers. I really wanted one of the lovely big stuffed animals that hung over the stands, but Uncle Jack said he'd rather buy one than waste more money on those crooks, the game was rigged. That sounded okay to me, even though I wasn't sure what "rigged" meant. Uncle Jack was such a good ballplayer that whatever he said was right with Davey and me.

We finished the day watching a man dressed in skinny plaid pants and pointed shoes throwing six pie plates in the air over and over without dropping one. For his "grand finale" he lit fire to a long sword, tipped his head back and, after a lot of drum noise, he slid the fiery sword down his throat 'til the handle touched his lips. I stood there with goose bumps. I couldn't swallow at all, my mouth was so dry. This had to be the bravest man in the world.

As we headed for home in the half dark, tired and dusty from a long afternoon, Uncle Jack picked me up and put me on his shoulders. The day was perfect.

The first day of school was coming closer. Alicia with Bum the cat came over announcing that she would show us how to get to school. Davey said he'd already found his way, it wasn't that hard. He didn't like Alicia that much, she was quite bossy and he didn't need a girl telling him what to do.

So, with Mama telling me to be careful, Alicia and I set off. We passed a lot of nice houses and Alicia told me names of kids who lived along the way. It really wasn't a long walk. Before I knew it, we faced a huge brick building, and Alicia, just like she'd built it herself, waved her arm announcing loudly, "There! That's it, your new school!"

My stomach started to hurt. This couldn't be a school, it was way too big and it looked scary. It was tall and dark, with more windows than I'd ever seen in one place. The door wasn't just a door, it was two, side by side. Nothing like my school in Altario, small and yellow, up on a hill so you could see it from our house. Nothing like my friendly school where I hung my coat in a cloak room with all the kids, where I had my own desk in the Grade

Mama

One row and Davey was just three rows over with the fourth graders. This couldn't be.

I turned around and started back. *Maybe I'll just go home and see Mama. She'll tell me it is okay. Maybe Alicia made a mistake, maybe she's not as smart as she always acts.*

But Alicia chased after me yelling, "What's the matter with you? Don't you want me to show you the grade two windows?"

"No, I've got to go home, I don't feel good!" I knew I was going to cry and I didn't want anyone but Mama to see me. I ran as fast as I could. Alicia, carrying big fat cat Bum, couldn't keep up. Mama was surprised to see me but, just like I knew she would, she put her arms around me and waited for me to tell her what was wrong. That was the nice part about Mama, she was always there and listened while my words tumbled out, holding me and brushing the hair from my eyes, making soft cuddly sounds.

I knew it. I felt better already. She made everything okay.

Joan Harder

Sunday Dinner

Monday through Saturday supper was the evening meal.
But the last meal on a Sunday had a very different feel.
Bacon and eggs for breakfast, then off to Sunday school,
Sunday dinner was at 4 and attendance was the rule.

Dad sat in his armchair at the table's end,
Mom, close to the kitchen, with food to attend.
Roast beef and gravy was always a winner
for me and for Davey, so we loved Sunday dinner.

Time and television make some meals
seem like an entertainment snack.
But I think I'd really like to have
my Sunday dinner back!

Triggered Memories: Rubber Boots

The other day I was on my porch preparing to trim the yard with the weed whipper. I was wearing a pair of old rubber boots to protect my legs from flying debris. For some reason those boots made me think of a time some seventy years ago.

After moving to Provost, Davey and I managed to settle into separate classrooms in that two-storey brick school that had seemed so huge. Our new home was a happy household, for now our dad was home for lunch and dinner each day. No more was he a traveller, away all week. Mama was happy and when Mama was happy the world was a wonderful place to be.

Winter was a great time for kids with lots of snow and places to sleigh ride. Best of all was the big outdoor skating rink across the street from our house. Daddy promised we would learn to skate. Although Davey and I had never had skates before, we'd often slid on an ice covered pond, so how different could it be? At the skating rink there was a warm change shack and a grandfatherly caretaker who helped tighten our laces and pick us up after hard falls.

Life was good. With the promise of spring's fresh warming air, we looked forward to whatever came next. But this spring, something was wrong. I woke in the night with pains in my legs that wouldn't go away and fevers left me bathed in sweat. The doctor came, and after examining me, he smiled, patted my cheek and said he needed to talk to my folks. I lay in bed listening to murmuring voices outside my door, catching words here and there, "Lots of bed rest, no excitement." Soon I heard the back door close.

Mama came back, smiled and hugged me, and said, "The doctor says you have rheumatic fever. To get better, you need to stay in bed for a long time and get lots of rest. His orders are for you to stay quiet, drink lots of water, eat your meals and take the medicine he left for you. When your legs hurt we'll rub them and keep them warm to make you feel better. It might take six weeks until you can go back to school."

The thought of missing six weeks of school didn't seem so bad at the time. My teacher had been a source of terror for me since the first day of school when she announced to my class, "I am much bigger than any of you. If you behave, we will get along just fine, but if not, I promise I will land on you!" So far I had not experienced the landing part, nor had I seen any of my classmates suffer this punishment, but her ominous words hung in the air like a dagger. *Smugly I thought, I won't miss that.*

For several days I was delirious and apparently entertained Davey with senseless ravings. These he gladly repeated to me in my lucid moments. The medicine I had to take was made tolerable by a beautiful big candy coated bubble gum the doctor brought on each of his daily visits.

As my fever subsided and pains in my legs lessened, days in bed felt long, but Mama did her best to entertain me with stories and songs. She had been a teacher so she helped me keep up with school work. Still, I longed to be outside, to follow rivulets of melting snow running down streets and to splash and play with my friends.

One morning after a miserable, sleepless night I opened my eyes. To my amazement, next to my bed was a pair of beautiful shiny black high top rubber boots. I never had rubber boots before, just overshoes that really didn't keep your feet dry. This year, I had to be careful to stay warm and dry so I wouldn't get sick again. The boots were there every morning when I woke up. They reminded me that I would get better. I tried them on many times before the day finally came when I could go outside again.

It was sometime later that I had a final check up at the clinic and heard the doctor say to my mama, "So often rheumatic fever leaves the patient with a serious heart defect. Fortunately, with your care, Joan's heart seems just fine!"

My First Quarantine

Our family had moved to Stettler, Alberta by the winter of 1941 when I became ill with scarlet fever. Only a few days later, Davey came down with mumps. At the time the local health unit required severe three week quarantines for both diseases. Warning signs were placed on our doors and no one but the doctor was allowed to leave or enter.

This came at a bad time for our family. First, it was the Christmas season. More importantly, my dad, once again a travelling salesman, was only home on weekends. To keep working during our quarantine he had to stay at a hotel in town, and only visited through the front door screen. It was a sad time for all of us, but especially for Mama. Dad did grocery shopping and errands and the doctor checked in on us. I was unaware of all of this for a while due to a high fever and bouts of delirium.

However, by Christmas Day, my fever had broken and Davey's swollen jaws were more normal. He and Mama decorated the tree and our living room was a bright festive place. Our mom was bravely doing her best to keep the spirit of the season, with the exception of tears when Daddy arrived at the door to visit. She set up a card table with a familiar red and green tablecloth and, somehow, under the tree there were brightly beribboned packages. I was happy that Santa had made his usual visit regardless of the signs on our doors. Luckily there was no sign on the chimney, at least, that was what Mama said. Christmas dinner was roast chicken with mashed potatoes, loads of dressing and gravy and NO turnips. The plum pudding with rum sauce was wonderful and we all talked with Daddy at the door. Mama said we should be thankful, and we were.

It seemed the quarantine would soon be lifted so life could go back to normal but, no, I wasn't feeling good. When the doctor came, he took one look and announced, "She has mumps." The sign stayed on our door for another ten days. This time we all cried. My mumps were mild and after tense days of waiting, miraculously, Davey did not get scarlet fever. The signs came down, Daddy came home and we were a family again.

When I look back and remember, Mama was in hospital the following Christmas. Her cancer had come back. Five years after her treatments on January 4, 1943, she passed away in my Daddy's arms.

Mama

It was December and there was lots of snow. Christmas was only a short time away, and though we had a tree, decorated and standing by the fireplace, it was all so wrong. There were only a few days left of school before the holidays. Today, when the bell rang at 4:00, Davey was waiting for me at the girls' entrance. He grabbed my hand when I came out and said, "We have to hurry, she'll be waiting."

We ran from the school yard down the street, hand in hand. Ahead loomed the big brick building that was the hospi-

Joan and Davey, Stettler, Alberta

tal. By the time we got there, my heart was thumping and I could hardly breathe. I think we were both a little frightened. We'd never been inside the hospital. They didn't usually let kids our age in to visit but as Daddy said, it was a special favor from the nurses because it was Christmas.

The nurse who met us inside smiled, said she had been expecting us, and asked us to follow her. The smell was different, a little bit like a doctor's office, but stronger. Lots of men and women in white were hurrying everywhere, pushing carts and carrying trays. We followed the nurse up a long, wide stairway and then down a hall with lots of numbered doors, some open, some closed. As we rushed along I saw glimpses of people in beds and some even waved as we went by.

Then our nurse stopped and said, "All right, we're here. You can stay until I come to get you. Remember you mustn't be too noisy." She opened the door.

There was Mama propped up on pillows, smiling with her arms open for us. Except she wasn't really like our mama, she was little and the skin on her hands and face was a strange yellow color and she looked as though she might break if I hugged her too hard. But it was Mama. Quickly Davey and I were in her arms and her hugs were Mama-hugs and her voice was Mama's voice and it didn't matter that she was small and yellow. She was Mama.

She wanted to know all about school, and what were we doing at the Christmas concert, and what did we want for Christmas? Oh, she was full of questions, and she laughed with us over everything. She proudly showed off a pretty new bed-jacket Daddy had given her, and she patted her hair just like when she was going to a party. She told us about all the new babies born that week and that one of them was a new sister for Helen Grey, a girl in my class. She even laughed and asked if we minded a Mama from China and we laughed too and said it was fine. Then, suddenly, the door opened, our nurse appeared and quietly said it was time to go. Mama gave us hugs and kisses and smiled and told us to be good for Aunty Ruby.

Davey said, "Daddy says you might be coming home for Christmas, Mama. Will you?"

She smiled again, "I'll really try." Her eyes were shiny and she blew us a kiss as the nurse closed the door softly and led us back down to the big main entrance.

The street lights were blinking on and snow was falling gently. Some of the houses had lighted trees in the windows and Davey held my hand again as we ran all the way home to tell about our visit.

Mama didn't come home for Christmas. On the night of January 4, 1943, Daddy opened my bedroom door and said quietly, tears streaming down his face, "We don't have a Mama anymore."

October

Whenever October rolls around and major league baseball fever heats up, my memory takes me back to my childhood. We had no TV, of course, but radio kept us in touch with the world. Every fall, everyone who knew anything about baseball had ears glued to their set, and it didn't matter what teams survived to make it to the final playoffs.

There were no Canadian teams in the major leagues but we didn't care. We felt connected to Yankees, Dodgers, Tigers, Cubs, White Sox, Red Sox, and Cardinals. As I recall, the biggest World Series battles involved the dreaded New York Yankees and a variety of brave, luckless "other guys." For some reason, underdogs always seemed to have my family's support. Back in the 30's and 40's (yes, that's with a 19 in front) the challenge to topple the intimidating Yankees made games much more exciting.

But, my favorite memory was 1945, the year the Detroit Tigers beat the Chicago White Sox. I can't pretend to remember player's names, but it was Thanksgiving weekend. After having stuffed ourselves with wonderful plates of turkey, stuffing, peas and mashed turnips (one tablespoon), gravy and pumpkin pie, we piled in the car for a drive.

The game was on the radio. The day was as perfect as you could wish. Trees still clung to their golden brown leaves, reluctant to let them go. Rolling farm fields boasted short yellow stubble like unshaven beards and flocks of geese in perfect vees followed their leader south to their promised land. There was a comforting drone of the play by play announcer. He described the game so vividly you could imagine being there, though it was a couple of thousand miles away in a city larger than any on the prairies. The patter between plays kept us involved along with the smack of the ball hitting leather and the umpire's calls,

"Steerike" or "Haw" or "Yer out." How the crowd roared when wooden bat and cow leather came together. You just knew fans were standing, wildly waving in excitement as if their cheers could send a runner all the way home.

Davey and I argued over which team we wanted to win, while Daddy tried to quiet us so he could hear.

Oh, it was a wonderful day. I could hardly wait to go home and gather kids on my street to choose sides for a ballgame of our own. Oh, yeah, and there'd probably be an argument over who got to be the Tigers.

A Christmas Memory

The winter of 1945 in central Alberta is a long way away and a long time ago but every year at this time pending Christmas celebrations force me to remember.

It was the last Friday before school holidays. Our grade eight class was finding the day intolerably long. We'd had a Christmas concert earlier and now just wanted out. Our teacher, Miss Gaspar, desperately tried to keep us busy, but was becoming visibly frazzled with the effort. School was not over until 4:00pm, still an hour away. Miss Gaspar suggested that, instead of our usual Friday spelling bee, it might be fun to hear how each of us found out that Santa was not real. One by one, down the rows, each student took their place at the front to tell their story. Because we felt so grown up, it was fun. Everyone seemed to be having a good time.

Everyone, that is, but Gertrude. Gertrude was taller than anyone else, she was a quiet girl, awkward and shy. We knew her family was poor because she and her younger sister wore the same clothes every day. Their shoes were so worn the backs no longer even covered their heels. They lived out in the country but no one knew where and it never seemed important to know. They walked to school every day. Their books were tied together with string, their lunch carried in a large covered jam pail with a wire handle. In winter they were always first to class. I had no idea how or where they lived or how they got to school on cold wintry days. They kept to themselves and we were content to let them.

But today, all eyes were on Gertrude. It was her turn to speak, but something was terribly wrong. Gertrude sat slumped at her desk, one finger twisting her long unkempt dark hair. A tear slowly made its troubled way down her cheek.

Miss Gaspar, never known for patience, urged her to stand. Slowly Gertrude rose and walked to the front. She turned to face us, her gangling figure the picture of dejection. She smoothed her skirt, lifted her shoulders and breathed in deeply. Then she raised her eyes and, staring straight ahead at no one in particular, she said quietly, "This is how I found out about Santa, here, today in class! Please don't tell my little sister, 'cause she doesn't know and she wants a blanket for her doll." Turning sharply, she squared her shoulders and left the classroom.

For a moment there was stunned silence, then giggles from the back row. Miss Gaspar's face had taken on a strange look, somehow it seemed crooked. It looked like she was going to say something but the only sound from her contorted lips was more like a cry. With one smack of her ever-present ruler against her desk, she silenced us. We had seen and felt that ruler at work. No one was about to take a chance with it now. With a withering glare that swept the room, she quickly left, close on the heels of the shattered Gertrude.

Since that was the last day before Christmas holidays, it wasn't until two weeks later that we were back in class. There were a few knowing grins and suggestive pokes as Gertrude, last to arrive for the very first time, took her seat. We'd exchanged holiday tales with friends in the school yard, but now, back in the familiar surroundings of the classroom, memories of our last day in class returned.

Miss Gaspar, however, had done her job well. During the holidays, a letter to our parents arrived. The true meaning of that incident was not to be ignored. Sometimes the lessons we learn come from unexpected places.

I pray that Gertrude's Santa came again that year.

A Christmas Story

When Mama's cancer returned, Daddy was still travelling for Massey Ferguson during the week. That was when Mama's younger sister Ruby left her job in Edmonton to care for all of us while Mama was ill but still at home. When Mama lost her battle with cancer, our Aunty Ruby stayed on to look after Davey and me.

Cliff and Ruby on their Wedding Day

Two years later, Ruby and my Dad married and we had a family again. That year Daddy announced it was high time we spent Christmas at "The Fort." He said it would be an adventure. The excitement was almost more than I could stand but it was scary too. I didn't ever remember spending Christmas anywhere but home. Davey and I had never made a winter trip to Papa and Grandma Dunc's.

The trip was not easy, roads north of Edmonton were poor and badly maintained. We bumped, slid and swerved our way, not without scary moments. It seemed we would never get out of the snowbanks but eventually we plowed through. At last we reached Athabasca River crossing, but there was no ferry. It had been pulled out of the water for the winter. The river was frozen over but the ice was not thick enough to support a car full of people. Instead a large box-like container hung from heavy steel cables reaching across the river. It was decided that Aunt Ruby, our new mom, Davey and I would go across in the "basket," while Daddy drove across the ice. The only one who thought this was a good idea was Dad, who just laughed at our fears, piled us into the hanging contraption and waved as we began our sliding ride to the other side. He lit up a cigarette, climbed in the car and drove out on the ice.

I'll never be sure which was scariest; rumbling across the wide Athabasca in the basket thing, or watching breathlessly as Daddy made his way slowly across the crackling ice below. But, of course I'm here, we made it, all of us. No disasters, no broken cables leaving us dangling precariously over the river, no gaping hole in the ice where once a car had been, none of the pictures that had flashed through my mind. In fact, it was kind of fun and what a story to tell the kids at school!

Grandma and Papa Dunc greeted us at the gate. Grandma was in her ever-present apron and Papa had a chew of tobacco firmly clamped between his teeth and cheek. Kissing Papa always left you with a little drop of tobacco juice on your cheek but I loved the smell of his pipe, which when not lit was usually parked in his shirt pocket.

We bundled into their warm, cozy farmhouse. The welcome aroma of stew wafted through the kitchen and the fresh scent of pine from the newly cut Christmas tree made the house a wondrous place. Soon, we were at a huge wooden table scooping great gobs of stew into big bowls, dipping thick slices of homemade bread into the dark, delicious gravy. Trials of the trip melted away with steaming bowls of Grandma Dunc's stew.

Christmas Day began with the happy arrival of Uncle Vic, Aunt Meatie, Uncle Maurice and our cousins. Though we only saw them once a year, our cousins were great fun. Soon we were making plans to go down to the creek to slide on ice under the bridge. Age didn't matter, we were just kids. Away we went down the hill with warnings to be careful following us.

There was only a skiff of snow on the ice, so we didn't waste time clearing it. With joyful abandon, we raced down the creek under the bridge, each of us trying to slide farther than the other. My first slide started out great, I really thought I was going to be the winner. But, before I could come to a victorious stop on the other side of the bridge, my feet stopped me. Suddenly I pitched face forward on the ice, no time to even put out my hands to save myself. Nope, I landed square on my nose and, unfortunately, my mouth was open. When I reached up to feel my face, my hand came away covered in blood. There, in the middle of a pool of red on the snow, was my front tooth!

Of course, that incident put a quick stop to my favorite Christmas festivities, except gifts, of course. I missed turkey, gravy, stuffing and grandma's wonderful suet pudding, chock full of candied cherries and nuts, covered with yummy hard sauce and rich rum sauce. My broken tooth screeched, "NO" when food or drink touched it. I would have to wait until we got back home to see a dentist. However, as long as I kept my mouth closed, something I was constantly told to do, outdoor fun was still great.

Anyway, it was all another super adventure with the usual twists and turns of a family Christmas!

Joan Harder

Dear Mom (to Ruby, written years ago)

What an understatement of undying, heart-wrenching love those words are!
If only just this once I can tell you feelings from years ago.
You took me in and never once let me see that I was not your very own.
Oh, I knew, of course, but you scolded, defended, nourished and ordered me
just like a Mom.
And just like a Mom, you had moments when you disliked me intensely.
When you desperately wanted to leave, to cast off these miserable, clinging kids you never bore, all the time sinking deeper and deeper into a family tie not really of your making.
But doing it, with grace and through self-sacrifice, still strong willed and true to yourself.
You saw us grow and bloom, I think. Off on our own trails, sometimes crooked.
And you had the joy of your very own, which I hope and pray you could love with abandon.
Your own from the very first instant. No one watching over your shoulder, yours.
And life was sweeter yet, with more sweetness to come.
Mom, take care, thanks for calling, come and stay, write, but most of all know how I understand you, and I love you.

The Honeymoon

Daddy and Aunty Ruby were older than many of their friends so they watched quite a few of Dad's younger buddies go off to war in the 40's. When Dad's friend Sam left, my folks kept in close touch with his fiancée Francis. Those years were lonely for Francis and for her friends with their boyfriends away at war so they spent many evenings at our home.

Fortunately, in 1945 when war ended, Sam returned safely. Their reunion was joyous and the happy couple decided not to waste another moment. About that time my family was about to go to Banff on a holiday. Sam and Francis thought it would be great to go away to marry rather than fussing with a large wedding. They couldn't afford a car yet, so arranged to travel with us to Calgary where they would marry.

Since little planning went into the event, once in Calgary Sam and Francis looked frantically for a minister. My dad, always one to take charge, helped with another oversight, the marriage license. Frances was almost in tears, but finally they found a reluctant minister and married with my parents as witnesses. (I don't remember what Davey and I did during the ceremony, possibly we waited in the car.)

We set off for Banff where the newlyweds hoped to find a cozy honeymoon cottage while we holidayed in the area. That summer Banff was a bustling town crowded with tourists eager to throw off their wartime woes. Accommodations were at a premium but after hours of searching my dad found a place. Sam and Francis, on the other hand, had no luck so were forced to share our rental. It had only one bedroom with a double bed and two cots, adjoined by an enclosed porch with two small couches. The honeymooners had to use the sun porch separated from us by two rather flimsy doors.

Being a little young to appreciate the frustration and inconvenience this caused the honeymooners, I remember being baffled, when in the middle of the night, I woke to a loud scraping noise from the porch. My brother and I jumped up to find our parents wide awake and laughing at the sound of two couches being shoved together on the sun porch. Sam and Francis were good sports. Hearing our laughter they joined in with their own and the giggling went on for some time.

This story made for great entertainment whenever Sam and Francis visited, which happened many times over the years.

That, except for my own, is the only honeymoon I was privileged to share.

The Day My Sister Was Born
April 27, 1946

The day had finally arrived. Ruby announced she was going to the hospital. The new baby was on its way!

There'd been a lot of preparation for your arrival. Both Grandmas vied for attention, making "old wives" predictions about when, where and what this new addition to our melded family would be. Grandma and Papa Dunc had arrived earlier and I had been regaled with stories of "birthings" Grandma attended as an unofficial midwife years ago down on the farm. Oh, she knew that wouldn't be her job for this baby. There was a hospital in Stettler and Ruby had been well looked after by Dr. Malcolm.

Dad cancelled trips out of town this week and was staying close to home. It had been a while since there had been a baby in this family and he was pretty nervous.

Grandma Thomas had been predicting a girl for some time, though no one really knew why. As the time for you to arrive came and went, she added the adjective "lazy" to her prediction. She said, "The baby was certainly taking its time getting here!" Whenever she said anything like that Papa snorted in disgust, scattering cigarette ashes in the air as he left the room. He didn't think Grandma was that all-knowing, but also figured there was no use arguing.

Davey and I were just excited at the thought of a new baby in the house, girl or boy.

Anyway, Dad took Ruby to the hospital, and promised to call us as soon as there was news.

75

In the meantime, the sky turned black and angry and the wind began to howl. Grandma Dunc, always a bit superstitious, worried this was not a good sign. She spent a lot of time muttering to herself as she went around the house closing windows. She told anyone who would listen to stay close, we were in for a storm. Right on target, the dust hit. The world turned dark as swirling dirt, leaves, and loose trash flew through the air.

I ran to the house for refuge and stared out the window waiting for the bad omen Grandma had worried about. I was nearly fourteen and felt quite sophisticated but Grandma Dunc always told such great stories. When she said something, I was pretty sure she was right.

While the storm raged, Grandma Dunc went calmly about the house with her dust cloth, wiping, rubbing and polishing everything in sight. It was almost part of her outfit, a dust cloth or dishcloth. It seemed she always flitted about cleaning like this. Papa Dunc would say, "For God's sake Mame, things just can't be that damn dirty. Put the cloth away for a while!" But that was Grandma, she was just a little bit of a thing with a thin face and graying hair pulled back in a bun. It seemed she just always had to be working.

Eventually the storm subsided and the sun came out shining over a world covered in a layer of dirt and grime.

No word from the hospital yet, but Grandma had a mission. Out she went, heavily armed with a broom, dustpan, scrub bucket and mop. Without a word she set to cleaning the front porch until it gleamed. Then, stopping only to change the water in her bucket, she attacked the front sidewalk. Not enough that she swept it clean, oh no, next she got down on her knees. Her house dress tucked up into her apron pockets, she scrubbed that sidewalk as though her life depended on it, all the time mumbling to herself. I know now it was her way of worrying and keeping busy kept her sane. Today psychologists probably have a name for her cleaning obsession but to us it was "just Grandma's way" and we loved her.

Not much later that day, Daddy called to say we had a new, pink, cuddly baby girl and they were going to call her Barbara. Barbara? I don't know if he ever said why but I guessed God thought it should be so. The excitement in our house was wonderful. Even Grandma and Papa Thomas smiled at each other and that didn't really happen that much. It was a truly wonderful day and now we could hardly wait to have you and your mom, our Ruby, home to complete the picture.

So, there you are, Sis. That's the story as I remember it, and I am still thrilled to have you for my baby sister. Love you so much.

Joan Harder

Thanks for Being You

Lucky, that's what I am, blessed with a Sis like you,
one who's thoughtful, generous and kind…and a little bossy too!
Sometimes I look back at our lives, and how we came to be.
Imagine, my sister's mom was my own Aunt Ruby!
A baby sister to show off, and sometimes pick on, too,
like when I cut your hair and made you cry,
I hate that I did that to you.
I do hope over all the years, you've forgiven me that stuff
'cause sometimes older sisters can be a little rough.
I love our phone call visits, there's always lots to say.
They make the miles disappear and brighten up my day.
And when the conversation ends with a quick last, "I love you,"
those words may seem just habit, but you know, I REALLY DO!

Joan and Barb, then and now

Aprons

Oh, yes, I do remember wearing aprons. Actually my grandmas called them "pinnies," which I guess was short for pinafore when I was a little girl.

However, my favorite apron was one my papa wore in his workshop. It wasn't very big, had only three pockets and tied around his waist. It was probably white when new but years of sawdust, glue, paint and varnish combined to give it a mottled puzzle of stains. The pockets bulged with a myriad of nails, screws, matches, small tack hammers, screwdrivers and, yes, even a small plane for shaving small wood pieces smooth. (That plane was my favorite of all his tools. Today I own one from Home Depot, along with my own carpenter's apron.) Deep down under all these was a collection of wood curls, scraps of cigarette butts and tobacco.

Papa was careful about disposing of his many cigarette butts. He never tossed a finished cigarette butt that might still smolder on the floor covered with wood scraps, but instead snuffed it out between his fingers, and stuck it in his apron pocket. Though I watched, waiting for his apron to start spewing smoke and flame, it never happened.

My papa had another apron, too, one that sat on top of their piano. That apron was emphatically off limits to anyone but Papa. In the desk drawer of our house there was another just like it and Mama told us we were not to touch it. Once a month the aprons went with my dad and my papa to their Masonic meetings.

Years ago, when I first came to Kingsville, I went to a church tea and bazaar. It was the 70's, the days of long skirts. I bought a black and white gingham ankle length apron to send to Barbara for Christmas. The last time I visited her home, I needed an apron. Barb went to a drawer, reached in and proudly handed me that same apron. It was a bit faded from many washings, but obviously it was a gift that kept on giving.

The Driving Lesson

This past summer I received the dreaded Ministry of Transportation letter reminding me I had to take a driving test to renew my license. It wasn't unexpected, it was the fourth I've had since turning 80. Although I have been a confident driver, somehow the idea of passing a test does cause some worry. Just the possibility of not being allowed to drive makes a cold lump form in my stomach. Losing the freedom to walk out of my home, jump (well, okay, crawl) into the driver's seat and set off for virtually anywhere, would create a large hole in my life. *Oh, I know the day will come. Deep down, I know I will cope, but it will take getting used to.* As it turned out, all went well on test day, I am still driving. But the whole thing triggered a memory that took me back 72 years to my first driving experience.

Although we had made a home in Stettler, I still missed people in my little hometown, so I was thrilled when Uncle Jack and Aunt Alla relocated closer to us. It was summer 1946 when my uncle asked if I would like to go with them on a weekend trip to Altario.

I was nearly fourteen, school was out, and I was bored. My friends were off to camps or cottages and a trip to Altario meant I would not be stuck doing nothing, at least for a few days. A family friend who owned the Altario Hotel had daughters I knew well so I was invited to stay. The drive was fun as my uncle was always full of stories and loved to sing. Because he and my aunt were great partiers, some songs were a bit raunchy. I tried hard to remember them so I could repeat them for my friends.

The weekend was everything I had hoped for and more. While my aunt and uncle partied with their friends, I was busy with my friends from the hotel. Both girls were a little older than me, but included me in all their plans. One of these, a big change for me, was a dance in a nearby town. The girls' brother, Alec, was old enough to drive so we piled into his old car and off we went. Now I was always a bit of a tomboy so dancing was not high on my list of things to do. Also, I was pretty backward when it came to boys but, hey, this was all new, I was going to make the best of it. Somehow the dance was a total surprise for me. As a new girl in town, I was instantly popular. I found myself with partner after partner, cute farm boys who really knew how to dance. What astonished me even more was, I didn't do badly myself! Anyway, in my eyes the dance was a huge success. As we left the hall and got in the car, I felt like Cinderella at the ball.

Sunday morning was quiet. The girls' chores had them cleaning in the hotel and dining room after a busy Saturday when farm folk came to town to get supplies.

We were to leave Sunday noon, but I hadn't seen my aunt or uncle. I was eating a late breakfast when my aunt came in, saying it was time to leave. As I followed her to the car I noted that she got in on the driver's side. This was a bit unusual, I'd never known my aunt to drive much. However, she told me to get in the front and as I did, I could see my Uncle Jack sleeping in the back seat.

My aunt seemed…not too steady. She giggled, "Jack is a bit under the weather." She would drive. I must have looked a little leery because she explained that the new car had an automatic gear shift and was easy to drive. Away we went down the road. In no time at all, I understood two things: really, my aunt could not drive, and certainly she was not sober. We swerved back and forth on the gravel road and suddenly she hit the brakes. We slid to a stop in the loose gravel. She turned the key and with a sheepish grin turned to me, "I guess you'd better drive."

I was stunned for a minute but it was clear that she was serious. Now the only time I was behind the wheel of a car I was a lot younger on my dad's knee. He guided my hands as I drove slowly around the yard. However, at this moment, I was pretty sure I could do a better job than my aunt. If I just went slowly I'd be okay, but then again Stettler was 140 miles away.

I got out of the car and we changed places. Uncle Jack snored drunkenly in the back, blissfully unaware. As I turned the key, the car jumped but luckily my foot found the brake and I knew the gear shift was in drive. Carefully I took my foot off the brake. We eased down the middle of the road. *If all went well I could stay in the middle and we'd be safe, unless we met another car. I'd worry about that when it happened.* Off we went.

After I safely maneuvered the first few curves and found the accelerator and brake pedal comfortably, I sped up a bit. By the time we were at the main highway I felt quite in charge. We rolled along carefully, staying well below the posted 50 mile per hour limit. My first challenge, meeting a car, was white knuckle. I slowly moved over, perilously close to the dreaded ditch. My hands hurt as I gripped the steering wheel like my life depended on it and, actually, I guess it did. I glanced anxiously at my aunt for reassurance as we met our first truck only to see her eyes closed. She dozed, apparently fully confident. How I wished I felt that way. I was relieved that there was little traffic that Sunday, except when we went through the town of Coronation. It seemed everyone in town was out, probably going home from church. I crept carefully through the streets praying I would not hit anyone trying to cross.

There were several smaller towns ahead but most were not on the highway. My biggest worry now was the gas tank. *What if we ran out of gas on a Sunday?* Listening to Dad I knew that service stations closed on Sundays and that it was damned inconvenient. *Oh well, the needle on the gauge seemed close to full. I would just have to hope.*

As the miles went by, my passengers continued to sleep in complete oblivion. By this time, I was actually glad I was in control. They were darn fortunate that I was with them on this trip! I had no way of knowing how long we were on the road, but was surprised to see a sign announcing Botha. I knew that we were only 10 miles from Stettler and home. Boy, would Dad be surprised when I pulled up to our house! No sooner had this thought entered my mind when there was movement in the back seat.

I heard my uncle's voice as he sat up and saw his chauffeur. "Jesus H. Christ! Stop the damn car!" I slammed on the brakes. Uncle Jack jumped out of the car, pulled my door open and yelled, "Good God Almighty! Get in the back seat, right now. Your dad will bloody well kill me if he sees you driving!"

Well, I loved my uncle, and I also knew not to argue. For the next 10 miles I pouted in the back seat. I couldn't help but think how lucky they were that I had taken such good care of them.

Drinking sure makes people difficult!

Normal Christmas?
(I don't think so!)

If you were a little kid living in a small prairie town in the 30's you probably thought Christmas started the day the Eaton's catalogue arrived in the mail. With its colorful shiny cover full of promise, it was a book of dreams we poured over for hours on end.

We pointed stubby little fingers at dolls that cried "Mama" and closed their eyes when they lay down and even wet their diapers after a bottle! Dolls that looked like Shirley Temple or Snow-White and even the seven dwarves! A train that you wound up puffed smoke around a track! There were toy telephones, wooden tinker toys with round wheels full of holes and sticks that fit in the holes so you could build wonderful things. Metal meccano sets with screws and nuts came with pictures to show you what you could build. Oh, the games we loved: snakes and ladders, pick up sticks, tic-tac-toe, dominoes, Chinese checkers with colored marbles! Ships that sailed in the tub and wind-up cars that would not fall off even when they got to the edge of the table. The wonders were never ending, or so it seemed to our bedazzled eyes.

Of course, these were the dirty thirties, difficult times for average families. Most kids just looked longingly at the wonders on those beloved pages. Only the luckiest might find a toy under the tree. More likely, on Christmas Eve they hung up their biggest sock and the next morning reached deep into the toe to pull out a Japanese orange or a delicious apple. Maybe ribbon candy too.

No thought was given to the fact that Mama gave up the idea of new stockings or that Dad forgot about the cigar he occasionally enjoyed. Fortunately Mr. McCullough didn't ask an arm and a leg for a nice big "tom turkey" for that fabulous dinner with all the trimmings followed by Grandma's famous mincemeat tarts and suet pudding.

As a child, I was unaware that everyone didn't have the kind of Christmas we had. Not until I was years older did I begin to appreciate my good fortune. And only much later did I hear stories of how folks coped in tough times while still reaching out to help others at Christmas.

Now, when I think back over the many many Christmases I have had, those that stand out in my memory are not the ideal we saw on Norman Rockwell's *Saturday Evening Post* covers. I remember the more unusual ones, like the Christmas Eve Dad arrived home late for dinner and was feeling no pain after sharing Christmas cheer at his office.

In those days, our house was heated with a space heater that used fuel oil. Dad filled it each night from a five gallon pail. That night though, he stumbled entering the kitchen and five gallons of smelly fuel oil gushed out over the shiny clean linoleum floor. I will never forget the look that flashed on Mom Ruby's face. Davey and I quickly disappeared upstairs to avoid whatever the result would be.

I can only speculate that my folks, without a word, spent most of the night sopping up oil with whatever material they could find. The house was so silent you almost heard snow falling. As I looked out my window the scene was a perfect Christmas card. I crawled into bed, pulled covers over my head and, without being reminded, said my prayers.

Next morning, Davey and I crept downstairs fearing the worst, but, although a rather strong odor of fuel still hung in the air, no other sign of the previous evening's disaster was evident. Our tree stood proudly in the living room corner, hovering over a pile of gaily wrapped gifts. Tinsel icicles shimmered in the lights. Stockings bulging with goodies left no doubt that Santa had made his usual visit. (When we were younger, we never questioned how he got in when we had no fireplace chimney. Now older and wiser, we were content to simply enjoy the fable.)

Papa Thomas, now a widower, now lived with us and shared Davey's attic room. Papa, who was very deaf, had slept soundly all night oblivious to goings on below.

Fortunately, my baby sister Barbara (or Babs as Dad called her), asleep in her crib in my parent's bedroom, was also blissfully unaware of anything untoward. Now she stirred, crying for her bottle.

The day was wonderful. Dad and Ruby had miraculously resolved problems of the night before, or at least they appeared to have declared a truce. Our turkey roasted in the oven and soon the delicious aroma emanating from the kitchen overcame any scent of fuel oil. The excitement of opening gifts quickly erased any further discord on the family scene. Peace reigned that Christmas Day in our home, at least for Davey and me!

If that jolly old fat man in the red suit was real, I'm sure that as he drove out of sight he would have exclaimed, "Merry Christmas to all and to all a good night!"

Newlyweds on the Move: Alberta Oilfields to Estevan Saskatchewan

My family had made their forever home in Stettler, Alberta. After renting houses for a time, Dad and Papa Thomas built a brand new home right behind the water tower just off Main Street. I completed my education in Stettler and made great friends. After graduation I worked as a teller in the local branch of the Royal Bank, following in the footsteps of Dave who also worked for that bank. (No longer did he go by "Davey.")

Then one day I happened to meet a young man named Walter Harder who worked in the newly formed oil exploration business. In 1953 we married. Walt's vocation in the burgeoning oil industry meant several, well, let's say many moves around Alberta. We accomplished these moves in a 27 foot trailer or as we preferred to call it "our brand new mobile home."

With the birth of our little girl Georgia all this travelling around became less appealing. So in 1955 we moved to Estevan, in southern Saskatchewan. We put down roots, first in our home on wheels in a mobile home park along the Souris River, and then in a basement apartment until we finished building our lovely home. Our family grew as we welcomed sons Seay and Mark. Estevan was a great place to raise a family, we lived there for eighteen years and were active in the community. Our children loved the outdoors and had freedom to enjoy it. Georgia rode her first horse there, we had two beautiful dogs, the boys played hockey and Walt hunted and fished.

It was in Estevan that I truly came into my own as a golfer, even winning the club championship in 1974!

Our First Move of Many to Come

There was definitely a storm brewing, not unusual on the prairies in January, but we set off on our journey anyway. We were young newlyweds with a brand new mobile home and this was our first move. It was 1954 and my husband was employed with one of many seismograph companies in business after Alberta's recent oil discovery.

We were leaving my hometown Stettler for Walt's job in Rocky Mountain House. Stettler had been my home for most of my life, so this was an adventure both exciting and scary. Before us was a journey of a couple of hundred miles and towing our trailer would be slow going. We were anxious to get an early start hoping to get there in daylight to find a space to park. My folks looked on worriedly as we waved goodbye and we were off.

This being my husband's first experience trailer hauling, we decided to take gravel back roads that would have less traffic and better traction. An hour or so later we came to grips with our error. Suddenly we hit a stretch of untraveled road and before we could stop, we plowed into a huge snow drift.

By this time the wind howled and snow swirled in all directions making visibility a serious problem. No amount of rocking back and forth resulted in moving ahead. Much to my distress, my husband decided to walk out to the highway for help. I was alone in the whirling storm but, worse, he would fight the wind and deep snow.

Time seemed endless, I was sure I would never see my husband again. *I would be found days later, frozen in the cab of our pickup.* I imagined more than one grisly scene. Our bodies were discovered, probably not before spring thaw since we hadn't bothered to leave word of our route. You read about things like that all the time on the prairies.

The truck was warm but I turned off the motor not wanting to be overcome by carbon monoxide even though I would eventually freeze to death anyway. I seriously considered following my husband's footsteps (non-existent by this time) despite my promise to stay put until he returned. Prayer seemed like a good idea. I hoped He was listening because I couldn't really remember my last talk with Him, and there might be a line-up for His attention that day.

For what seemed like hours I stared, nose pressed against a rapidly frosting window, seeing nothing but a white wall that created a dome of silence over our truck. So intent was I on my imagined tragedy, alone there in the howling blizzard, I didn't hear the sound of a motor approaching. So, when suddenly a hooded face appeared in the driver's window, I shrieked with shock. He was covered with snow, eyebrows white with frost, cheeks red with the cold but his grin was familiar. I was overcome with relief as my husband hopped in the cab. Proud of his efforts, he obviously enjoyed the look of disbelief on my face.

Suddenly I felt warm all over. *How could I have doubted that he would be back?* After all he was strong, had a great sense of direction and spent a lot of time outdoors. Luckily we had become stuck near a crossroad. After he trekked a mile through the storm my husband came across a service station on the adjoining highway. With a keen sense of direction he had indeed found help.

Before long, a tow truck pulled our rig out of the deep snow. Not taking any more chances, we headed for the main highway.

The storm subsided as we pulled into Rocky Mountain House. Sun broke through clouds to glisten on snow-capped mountains hovering in the distance beyond the foothill town. What a welcome sight! It was too late to find a place to park our little home but tomorrow would be fine. Tonight a nice supper, a hotel room and hot bath would be more than welcome.

No trailer park was available so we found a family willing to allow us to park in their driveway and to hook up to their power. For a fee we arranged to share bathroom facilities with the family, a new experience for me. I didn't really like the idea.

However, like it or not, this was a taste of life on the move. Our sojourn in Rocky Mountain House was brief.

To Georgia on Her Birthday

I have been sitting here at my computer remembering the day you were born. At that time we lived in Stettler in our mobile home parked in Papa Cliff and Grandma Ruby's driveway, right behind the water tower on Main Street.

The night before you were born I experienced what I thought was indigestion. Papa and Grandma had been out but when they came home about 11:00pm they stuck their heads in our door to check on me since you were due any day. When I told Grandma I was suffering from indigestion she just grinned and said, "Uh huh, that's what you think!"

Your dad and I played a game of scrabble and went to bed for what turned out to be a short night. Shortly after midnight it became quite apparent this was going to be a very big day.

My suitcase had been packed for a day or two, rather odd for me, a last minute type of person. But this wasn't an everyday occurrence. By this time you were getting pretty demanding. The pains began to affect your dad almost as much as me. I've heard a lot of women say that their husbands were overcome with remorse as their wives experienced labor pain. It's funny, but I thought it was more the mystery of it all and the fact that they were left out of things just at the most crucial time in such an amazing process. Anyway, it certainly is different now. Dads are totally involved and feel so much more important in their roles.

But, to get back to you. Fathers were not allowed in the delivery room and not encouraged to hang around, so your dad went home to a sleepless night. I spent the next few hours walking around and around the delivery room, talking a lot to myself and a lot to God. I wanted you to be born healthy and I wanted you to be born…SOON! And I didn't want to think about any additional members in our little family for a long, long time.

You arrived healthy and hollering and I was so proud I had stayed alert to hear your first cry. You were beautiful, even then. Dad was so proud of you and thought you definitely looked like his side of the family. He chose Georgia for your name after an old family friend from Iowa who was quite a lady. I never met her, but her name was Georgia Tripp. Then we had to have a middle name. Though Dad thought Joan was best, I chose to use the last part of my first name Evelyn because I wanted your name to flow easily. We agreed, you were Georgia Lynn.

At that time new mothers and babies stayed in hospital for ten days. Imagine, today it's 24 hours to 3 days. Ten days was unbearably long. I wanted so much to take you home and for us to start to be a family. And of course to show you off, as only your daddy and grandma were allowed to visit the maternity ward. Papa Cliff, Barb, John and my friends stood on the hospital grounds below my window and I held you up so they could see you.

What a day it was when we came home from the hospital. You were placed in a brand new carriage with a removable basket. That basket doubled as your bed for your first months. When you were one month old we moved to Innisfail, Alberta, with you in that basket tucked neatly between dad and me in the front seat of his pickup truck.

That was the first of many moves. I must tell you, shortly after, on our next move, we carefully packed the trailer, unhooked the propane and hopped in the pickup. As we started off, we looked at each other and almost in harmony said, "My God, Georgia is still on the sofa!" It was the first and last time we made that mistake!

Well sweetie, it's lovely to think back to those times and although we have seen a lot of changes, you remain constant, caring and loving and you are so loved. This summer's reunion was even better than I could have hoped. It was a thrill to see all those little bodies hanging on fences checking out farm animals. What a perfect place you and Stan have built and what a great job you did to make our gathering such a success.

Thanks so much for always being there. When we talk on the phone with a coffee close by it's the next best thing to being with you. Have a wonderful birthday, give yourself as many hugs as you possibly can. I love you so very much. XXOO Mom

Oil Wives International

As newlyweds the only home we knew was our 27 foot trailer, but we agreed it was beautiful. It was more beautiful because Walt had sold his very first car, a shiny black '52 Ford to make the purchase. With a home on wheels we could follow Walt's work. There were several moves in our future, actually this proved to be an understatement…we moved twelve times in the first year of our marriage!

Packing up was an exercise we learned the hard way, when, after our first move from Rocky Mountain House we unlocked the door to a disaster. Broken dishes, pots and pans, groceries, spilled milk and much more covered the floor. This was not only a big clean up job but a true test of our ability to laugh at ourselves. How naïve we were but we learned quickly. From then on cupboards were stuffed with pillows, doors securely taped, fridge defrosted and emptied and breakables carefully packed. We became experts in this game.

Three weeks later we were on the move again, much wiser and slightly less excited about the life of a "doodlebug" as they called us in those days. Very soon it dawned on me just how small our home was, especially in the middle of a western winter. I spent so much time alone. Most towns we arrived in were completely unprepared for an influx of "trailer folks." Very few mobile home courts existed and most often we knocked on doors to find someone willing to have our little home parked in a driveway or backyard. We were dependent on hooking up to their power and, when possible, water. We often had to share the homeowner's bathroom or, worse, only have access to an outhouse.

Sharing bathrooms had complications. We watched for our landlord's family to leave for work or school before we shyly ventured forth for our own needs, a roll of toilet tissue tucked under one arm and a bag of supplies on the other. We paid well for these privileges and it was an exciting day when the house was empty for a few hours. Then I filled the bathtub with warm suds, and thoroughly enjoyed a soak, singing at the top of my lungs. And I prayed I wouldn't hear a door open while I was in full song.

Except for a few other wives whose husbands worked in the same seismograph "party" it was difficult to make friends. We were always on to the next assignment. The men worked long hours, at times staying nearer a job in mobile bunkhouses. It was common to keep meals warm or cook in the middle of the night. Nothing in our life was routine and I began to look forward to moves that brought us closer to Stettler. I yearned for wonderful family visits and a chance to share coffee and giggle over stories with girlfriends there. Walt joked that I could be ready in half an hour when we moved closer to Stettler. He was right, I longed for the warmth of family and friends.

After three years, our gypsy style life definitely lost any appeal. We had our little Georgia, not quite two, when Walt took a permanent job with a pipeline company in Saskatchewan. We packed our trailer home and the three of us headed for the latest hotbed of the oil industry in Estevan, hundreds of miles away from Stettler and my family. It was a new adventure, though, and we looked forward to it.

Estevan was a larger town than we had ever lived in and thankfully had a well-established mobile home court on the outskirts of town, overlooking the wide Souris River Valley. The view was grand in the spot we found near the valley edge. Letters home were filled with glowing descriptions of our new surroundings.

Our trailer was small compared to those around us, obviously these folks weren't about to pull up stakes. We hooked up to power, water and sewer service and were on top of the world. We were finally able to live in our own home without depending on anyone else and, the best part, we used our very own bathroom! Admittedly it was tiny, one needed to decide before entering just what the plan would be. The tub was short, only accommodating a seated position, but there was a shower and I loved it. Georgia's crib fit neatly between our bed and the bathroom wall. There was a place for everything, if only we put it there! There was even a full length mirror on one of the closet doors. That closet was filled to capacity and on several occasions the door would pop open. Not a problem during daylight, but a scary thing when, in the dark on the way to the bathroom, one encountered a filmy-gowned figure face to face. Once when my uncle came to stay it so startled him that he hit the mirror in self-defence and woke everyone as he shouted one of his favorite obscenities.

The oilfield industry was relatively new here too. Sleepy little towns never anticipated droves of workers pouring into their unsuspecting midst; pipeline layers, geophysical engineers, surveyors and truck drivers. Nor did they expect the families who needed places to live. Businesses were springing up and down Main Street with little thought to planning. Welding shops next to homes, restaurants, coffee shops, oil field service companies and office buildings all rushed to open for business. Stores had never been so busy and money had never been so good. In a way it was a small version of the gold rush era. Our new town, known only for coal mines, bustled like never before and although the economy was booming, people seemed to resent the intrusion. It often seemed as if we existed on the outer edge of society.

It was lonely sitting in that little mobile home, especially when hot, dry days of summer and intense prevailing winds made just moving seem a cruel chore. On a lot of days, oh how the dust blew, sneaking like an unwelcome trespasser into every opening or crevice until everything one touched was grit. No relief from the heat, no welcome draft from an open door. Picnics at the river took the place of supper. Trees along a running river were an Eden in the middle of the God forsaken prairie.

The movie theatre, we discovered, was air conditioned. It was an unheard of luxury, and our salvation on hot summer days. Failing that, the drive-in theatre was a welcome breath of fresh air on nights when sundown didn't make a difference and our little home refused to cool.

We developed a routine that first summer. Movies changed every two or three days so alternating between drive-in and theater we saw nearly every show that came to town. Our little girl was accustomed to falling asleep even during the most exciting car chase, gun fight or love scene and always enjoyed the popcorn.

The feeling of not belonging began to fade when a neighbour invited me to an Oil Wives International meeting. The club was chartered to fill the needs of women whose husband's petroleum industry careers took them anywhere in the world. That night I met a host of friendly well-traveled women of all ages and learned of their dinner dances, stage shows, golf tournaments, bridge clubs, curling bonspiels and charity work.

For $1.50 to cover dinner and hall rental, my life changed immensely.

Seay

I awoke on that cold snow-covered Monday morning exhausted and strangely disappointed. My eyes roamed the small cozy bedroom to assure myself that I was in the right place. Next I glanced at the sleeping figure beside me. Then a vaguely familiar twinge brought my attention to a substantial mound under the covers filling the space between my head and my feet. I was nine months pregnant and today was going to be the day.

I lay there gathering my thoughts and wondering why, on such a wonderful day, I should feel a sense of frustration. Slowly it came to me. All night long I had the same recurring dream. Again a twinge, stronger this time. My dreams had been interspersed with beginning contractions that were quickly becoming those dreaded but also welcomed labor pains. Only in my dreams I had already given birth to a lovely baby boy and was relishing the joy of a job well done when I awoke.

"Oh, no! I have to do it all over again!" I moaned as another contraction sent all other thoughts out of my mind and straight to my mid-section.

The sleeping figure next to me rolled over, staring at me with a puzzled expression. He struggled to surface through the heavy weight of sleep pinning him to his pillow. "Do what over again?" he mumbled, raising up on one elbow and fixing me with a questioning look. "What's going on?"

I reached over and took his hand, placing it on my hilltop of a stomach just as another wrenching contraction moved under his hand. Suddenly Walt was wide awake. His eyes lit up with excitement as the full realization of what was going on hit him. "This is it? You're in labor? How long do you think?" He gingerly removed his hand from my stomach, as though the weight of it could possibly do some harm.

Seeing the happiness on his face, I felt warm all over. And somehow superior because this was going on in my body. For the most part, everything I felt would remain a mystery to him no matter how I tried to describe it. Yet, in a way it was sad that this oh so special time couldn't be completely shared with the person who made it possible.

Another contraction quickly reversed those loving thoughts. *Oh, God, if you only knew what hell I'm going through, if your belly was home to a twisting, turning, larger than life piece of humanity who will make the next several hours seem like days.* Now the joy on his face had taken on a look of panic and, yes, fear so those words stayed as thoughts in my head. The pain subsided and I was able to think again. *It's not his fault that God's procreation plan is perverted and totally unfair. Maybe God really is a man. That sure would explain it.*

My emotions tumbled head over heels from elation (between contractions) to regret (*Why, oh, why did we think one child wasn't enough?*) and back again, flip flopping like a slinky on a wooden stairway. Then, as I heaved my overburdened body to the edge of the bed, it dawned on me. The pain was less intense. I noted the time on the nightstand. Sitting on the bedside waiting for the next one to start I realized that, until now, I had paid very little attention to the intervals between.

I stared at the ticking clock while Walt slid by me and out of bed. "I'd better call the office and let them know I might be late. Have you got your suitcase packed? Where's the toothpaste?"

I dragged my eyes away from the clock and answered, "In my suitcase, you'll have to buy more. Don't forget to put it back in my case. Funny, the pains seem to be gone and the last ones weren't that strong." I felt a sudden disappointment. Now that I had accepted the fact that today was Baby Day, I sure didn't want it to stop. It was a full half hour before I felt the familiar deep squeezing pain again, then nothing. I was angry and wanted to blame someone for this come-and-go party going on in my mid-section.

Walt dressed quickly and made toast. "No I can't eat a thing." I wanted to cry. "Just go to work, everything's stopped. I'll get Adeline next door to take me to the hospital and she can call you when I get there." The way things are going, maybe I'm just having another dream. The disappointment was more than I could bear.

Walt questioned the wisdom of leaving and said, "Why don't I take you to the hospital right now and then you'll be there if it starts again?"

"Oh, sure, they're not likely to admit me when I'm not having any pains at all, and I'm NOT!" It wasn't his fault, but I wanted it to be. After all, he was the only one there.

He muttered something comforting, patted my shoulder and left confused.

I watched as exhaust from his departing car left a frozen trail in the air. As he drove down the street and out of the mobile home court my heart sank. Why did I let him go when I needed him? By this time, three year old Georgia was awake and came sleepily into the kitchen. Momentarily I was overcome with the joy of this beautiful little bright eyed girl who had stolen our hearts so completely. I scooped her clumsily into my arms and collapsed on the sofa with the effort. We lay there giggling and cuddling. "Know what, I think your baby brother or sister is going to come today. What do you think of that?"

Suddenly the world was okay again and whenever this lump inside me decided to make a move, I'd be ready. I poured milk on Georgia's cereal, put on a pot of coffee and called my neighbour. Adeline was young, newly married and she adored our little girl. She was lonely and our daily coffee chats made our lives brighter. Also, she had a car and was a willing chauffeur when I needed one. This hopefully would be one of those days.

It wasn't long before I got my wish. The contractions started with a vengeance, this time regular with a few minutes between. The secretary at Walt's office informed me that he had made an emergency trip to the field but promised to call soon. Soon wasn't good enough. With

Georgia in tow and full of questions, Adeline packed us in her car and we headed for the hospital. She would contact Walt and care for Georgia until he came home.

At the hospital nature picked up the tempo and my labor progressed as though there had been no stop. Adeline wished me luck, leaving me in the capable hands of the maternity nurse. There were forms to fill out. "Can't we do this later or when my husband comes?" I begged the dour nursing sister at the desk. But no, everything had to be in proper order. *What the heck is proper order when you're doubled over, hanging on for dear life to that demanding person inside that wants to be out? Insanity in the family you ask? Could you doubt it, would anyone in their right mind do this on purpose? Oh, God, oh God, you've gotta help me, I can't do this on my own!*

Then mercifully there was a wheelchair and for the next multitude of minutes, hours, what seemed like a lifetime, there were only voices ordering me to do this, don't do that yet, yes, yes, we'll give you somethingggg...

"Mrs. Harder, you have a beautiful baby boy, and he's a big one. He's got all his fingers and toes and the other stuff and, yes, your husband is on his way."

I saw the little bump wriggling in a blanket next to me and drifted off into the restful satisfied sleep that would be my last for many months to come.

January 27, 1958. Welcome to the world, Seay.

Joan Harder

Seay with mobile home in background, Estevan, Saskatchewan

Kindergarten Graduation Day, 1960

It was late June 1960. I groaned as I rolled out of bed to face the day. Our five year old was graduating from kindergarten today and there was to be a picnic lunch at a park by the Souris River. Our little graduate was already up, dressed in her favorite sundress and busy telling her younger brother Seay what a fun time we were going to have.

I smiled as I chose a comfortable outfit. I managed to stuff my swollen feet into a pair of loafers, these being the only shoes I could wear now. I moved my nearly nine month pregnant self through the motions of getting ready and tried to match the enthusiasm of my two happy kids. A new member of our family was due to arrive in a couple of weeks and I was HUGE.

However, I didn't want to disappoint Georgia, so off we went to the park. Everything went well. The food was great, the watermelon was cold and all the kiddies had a wonderful time. Mrs. Adams, the kindergarten teacher had outdone herself planning games and entertainment. So far, no one had skinned a knee, spilled their pop or lost a hotdog in the coals. More importantly, the river was far away so it was possible to keep an eye on everyone. I had somehow found a comfortable perch.

Then it happened. Mrs. Adams announced there were a few prizes left and it would be fun if the mothers competed for what turned out to be oversized Oh Henry chocolate bars.

Now, nothing was a more favorite treat for my Georgia than chocolate bars! After a couple of moments of pleading, I agreed to join the game whatever it might be. Well, the game, it turned out, was fairly simple for most but for someone in my condition it was a touch more challenging. The idea was this. Each mom would remove her shoes, and place her left shoe on the front part of her right foot. The object was to kick the shoe as far as possible and the longest kick would win the big bar.

Georgia was jumping with anticipation and knew her mom would be best. I melted. Any idea of backing out disappeared in the face of her belief in me. I stepped to the line and heaved my right leg as hard as I could, flinging that loafer far out into the trees. The pain that shot through my lower body took my breath away. I sat down on the nearest bench with a thump.

There was no doubt Georgia's faith in me had been sustained and the chocolate prize was ours!

With help from concerned mothers and the astonished teacher, my shoes were retrieved. Any thought of putting them on was out of the question. Georgia and Seay happily argued about fair sharing of the Oh Henry as we slowly made our way to the car and home.

Yes, I was a winner but for the next two weeks I could not lift my feet off the floor. I shuffled everywhere. My doctor was kind enough to be sympathetic, but warned me the upcoming delivery would be considerably more difficult due to pulled pelvic muscles.

As a result, on July 4th, the day of our youngest son Mark's arrival, I was blissfully unaware thanks to a strong dose of anaesthetic. I will say that he was well worth waiting for.

It was several weeks before the muscles I had damaged began to repair.

I never wore those shoes again.

Mark, on your 50th Birthday

I remember vividly the day you were born. As a matter of fact, you could have been born an American. The day before we went shopping in Crosby, not expecting your arrival for a few days.

Dad drove me to the hospital early in the morning. You were not too long in making your appearance, shortly after 10:00am. You were such a healthy beautiful baby with just a smidgeon of dark hair and smooth creamy skin.

Dad took holidays, staying home to look after Seay and Georgia and while I was in hospital Aunt Rena and Uncle George arrived for a short stay. Your dad was very grateful for their help with cooking and laundry.

A couple of days after you were born Georgia and Seay came with Dad to the hospital where he parked the car below my window so I could wave to them. That day

Walt and our kids

he brought me a beautiful bowl of Saskatoon berries and cream. It was a hot day so that was a fantastic treat. While I was enjoying the berries there was a stir in the hallway and there in the doorway was your two year old brother. Kids weren't allowed in the maternity ward but Seay, even then, in spite of Georgia's protests, was determined. He walked in, went up the elevator and told the nurses he wanted to see his mother and brother. They didn't have the heart to turn him away but he didn't get to see you until we brought you home. You were never far out of his sight after that. You became his special charge. Georgia mothered you and you were the easiest baby. Every day was a delight.

Sometimes when I look at the person you have grown to be, bright, ambitious, with a family you are proud of and a busy successful career, I see you still hold lots of hopes and dreams. I see glimpses of the boy who loved to be active and on the go, brown and busy, phoning home to let me know (true or not) where he was and what he was doing.

I love you Mark, I am proud of the man you are and I wish you nothing but happiness and health for years to come.

Grasshoppers

There it was on my pen, peering up at me with big unblinking eyes. The brightest green grasshopper I've ever seen. He (I'm only guessing) seemed unconcerned, though I'm sure he wasn't in the habit of sitting on a desk. I think he was as surprised as I was. I lifted him gently, opened the door, and set him free to join the rest of his grasshopper friends wherever they were.

Oh, I know there are other names for the busy critters, mainly locusts I guess, but where I come from they are grasshoppers, a very good descriptive name. What better way is there to describe an insect that lives in and on grass and has an amazing ability to hop? Actually, they do also fly and can travel in rather large hordes.

If you are expecting a scientific diatribe with Latin names and variations of the species, read no further. This is simply a story about my experiences with grasshoppers.

On the prairies I grew up in the "dirty thirties," years of drought that caused farmers to migrate hoping for a kinder place to settle. Grasshoppers too tend to look for greener areas but somehow they were remarkably prolific during that time.

I particularly remember how painful it was to stretch outside the car window in summer, hoping for a cooling breeze, only to be jolted by sudden sharp pain as a hopper collided at full speed with the bare flesh of my face or arm. This generally prompted competition with Davey to see how many we could snatch out of the air. The contest kept us occupied travelling down dusty roads on Sunday afternoons with our parents. They never minded the sport, it was far better than listening to our more common arguing or scrapping over space in the back seat.

I'm sure Davey won the number count as he could reach farther out the window than I could.

Years later, living in a mobile home at an Estevan trailer park, summers were again hot, dry and dusty. As for me, I hated the grit and heat but kids always have had a wonderful ability to adapt. They simply enjoyed life, wading in the river and thinking of all kinds of novel entertainment with kids in the park.

One day when I went out to check on my children I discovered a number of huge grasshoppers, each easily three inches long, hopping about near the hitch of our home. I wondered why they didn't fly away. To my amazement, I saw they were tethered on leashes of thread attached to the hitch. The kids had decided to make them pets, and took them for walks! I must say I was proud of their ingenuity and after all, they did free their pets each day, finding new replacements the next morning.

Years later, having grown to a family of five, we were building a house. Our neighbours in the subdivision had just put in a lovely new lawn. It was coming along beautifully, lush, green, about three inches high. While having coffee with my neighbour we admired the new growth.

The next day, I returned to the subdivision to do some painting and could not help but notice that our neighbour's lawn was now bright yellow. But it was a yellow that seemed somehow to be moving. On closer inspection, the entire lawn was a mass of hungry grasshoppers devouring new growth. According to my friend, they came over the back fence en masse, moving through the yard systematically gorging on grass. I still remember what an awesome sight it was but, of course, heart breaking for our neighbours, who were left with nothing but an expanse of bare soil with a few sad sprigs here and there.

I lived in Estevan for many years, but never saw a horde like that again. I have heard that locusts tend to live and move in cycles and if that's true, I'm happy not to have seen their next great emergence.

Memories of Georgia

From the time she was able to talk, Georgia quickly learned to say "horsie" and pointed excitedly at horse pictures in her favorite books. Auto trips were interspersed with stops to take a closer look at whatever equine shape appeared. Georgia just loved horses.

Her own first horse was one lovingly built by her dad when she was 2 ½ years old. It was a big-eyed teasing pony on rockers.

Georgia rides her rocking pony built by Walt.

Unfortunately this pony, ridden wildly for several years by a vast array of little folk, never survived to occupy a place of honor in some little child's room. But, as though it were yesterday, I can see that pony and the little girl who rode him so hard.

Georgia has long since moved on to ride real live horses with great skill, this love of her life never having changed.

In Estevan, Georgia's first horse was a feisty bay we christened Jazz. She had a prima donna attitude that intermittently brought tears of frustration and rushes of joy. She never sold her favors for a pail of oats. In the six years she was Georgia's horse Jazz never became easy to catch, less spirited, or fond of men in hats. Nor did she fall for the usual treats associated with horses such as apples or sugar cubes. As a result, Georgia learned never to take a four legged animal for granted and she is probably wiser for it. I can speak from experience as I spent more than a few hours begging, chasing and cornering Jazz. At times I even crawled through long grass hoping to catch that crafty animal off guard long enough to slip a halter over her beautiful head.

Since Jazz, there have been many horses in Georgia's life and there will be many more. But I'm sure there has always been a special place in Georgia's heart for her first horse and the memory of that joyful, tearful moment when she realized her little girl dream.

Whiskers

It was a wicked wintry day in southern Saskatchewan. The wind howled like a lonely coyote as snow pelted sideways against windows making the outside world an unfriendly frigid place.

It was Saturday. Normally my three active kids would have been bundled up, happily sledding on the hill conveniently located at the end of our crescent or playing road hockey on the quiet street. However, with the thermometer dipping close to 30 below that wasn't happening today.

Fortunately cable TV had recently become available. After some financial soul searching, and a lot of pleading on the part of the kids, we succumbed to the temptation. I figured I would let Donald Duck, Mickey Mouse and Superman do their thing on the big box while I went about my usual bed making and picking up chores.

Later we'd bake cookies, something the kids loved and so did I. They liked cookies but also loved to hear me do my Madame Jeanne Benoit imitation. It fulfilled a part of me that loved hamming it up and the kids were a great audience. The Madame, a chubby cute little French woman, had a TV cooking show. As she prepared her many recipes, she carried on a delightful running dialogue, all with a heavy French-Canadian accent that I loved to imitate.

For now, the kids were happily lined up in front of the TV. They munched on overloaded bowls of Captain Crunch. They were eating it dry so they could stare at the latest duck exploits without missing a bite and dribbling wet cereal on the carpet. My idea, not theirs!

Suddenly I sensed that the cartoon sounds and giggling had stopped. Quiet in our household was generally only a good sign late at night after everyone was asleep. So, with the normal suspicion of a mother, I headed for the living room to check things out. The TV was off. All three kids were lined up at the window, noses to the glass (*oh happy day*), staring out intensely.

As I entered the room, the three turned as one body. In a perfect chorus they hollered, "Mom, can we keep it? Please, please! He looks so little and so cold and hungry."

I looked out to see what "it" was and there, huddled below the window, was a dark grey ball of snow-flecked fur with two bright eyes and a little mouth that was obviously begging the audience inside.

Now we had never had a cat, and with good reason. That reason was my husband, who seriously considered getting a dog (hunting variety, of course). But a cat was out of the question, no discussion, "Thank you very much!" It was pretty well understood that Dad held the power in discussions of that kind. As a child, my dad held the same opinion about feline pets, so it appeared to me reasonable, or if not reasonable, just the way it was.

This could be a very long day. It seemed the decision would be all mine as inclement weather did not daunt Walt when there was a problem at the Midale pipeline terminal. The kids never tired of saying, "Daddy, do you have to go to 'Yourdale' again?"

Anyway, the fate of this little beast was in my hands, and at present the scale certainly tipped in the feline's favor. I didn't want to appear a pushover, though, and needed a defence, however weak, when their dad arrived home. I said, "You know that is just not possible. Besides, he's probably got a home close by, he's just lost. In the meantime take him to the garage and give him bread and milk. I'll call the neighbours to ask."

This, of course, was met by a chorus of, "Mom, no one on our street has a cat!" which was true, I knew. I could see by their faces that a chink in my armor showed, but the next battle had to wait. The boys grabbed jackets, raced to the door and left their sister to get a saucer and milk. *Even then, women's work.* I smiled to myself.

The kitten offered no resistance. I watched as the boys argued over who would carry and who would open the garage door. Four year old Mark got door duty, and in they went. I felt secure in my decision, silently hoping that before "Can we keep it?" began again their dad would have arrived. The situation would then be out of my hands. *Yes, I admit, I was a coward.*

Too soon Mark came in, close to tears. "We have to bring him in the house, it's really cold out there. Georgia says he'll freeze and die!" There they were, tears ambling slowly down those rosy cheeks I loved, and once again my resolve weakened. *Where was that man?* I knew he needed to come home, and be the "Bad Guy" who saved me!

The storm raged on. No company car pulled into the driveway as it quickly filled with snowdrifts (dairy queen cones we called them). I never did make the decision. By this time Georgia, jacket off and wrapped around the kitten, was inside the door with Seay close behind. From then on, it was clear to me we were going to have a cat. The look of love and caring on the faces of those three kids was enough to overcome arguments, cat haters and allergies, whatever!

There were some loud discussions with their dad. And repeatedly I heard the exaggerated refrain, "But Mom said we could." In the end, it was a done deed. No calls to neighbours asking if they knew of a missing kitten. A few recriminating looks were directed at me, but all in all, it was a rather simple transition from no pet family to home for Whiskers.

One rule, however, was demanded by their father. "The damned cat stays OUT of the living room and OFF the beds or he's a goner!"

Now cats are not that easy to control, especially a tomcat with a mind of his own. Even though four out of five family members obviously exhibited poor pet discipline, one thing amazed me about Whiskers. Although he often slunk past me to the living room sofa, found his way to a kid's bed, or occasionally into an open bureau drawer, the minute the company car pulled in the driveway, that cat suddenly appeared in the kitchen. There he calmly cleaned his paws with a look of innocence that I would have loved to be able to imitate.

Joan Harder

Christmas Poem 1972
(on homemade card sent to relatives)

The other day, we went downtown, some Christmas cards to buy.
We looked at all the different kinds, but found the price too high!
So here, on dirt cheap paper, with scissors and some glue,
is our Merry Christmas message, especially for you!

Since last you had some news from us, the temperature has dropped.
The golfing and the swimming have definitely stopped.
Walt took his trusty shotgun and went out after pheasant.
Some of them were careless, they tasted very pleasant.

We tried out one mixed bonspiel in another bid for fame.
It turned out not too badly; we only lost one game.
We rooted for the Roughies in the Hamilton Grey Cup.
The Tigers didn't eat 'em raw, but they sure did chew 'em up!

Our Georgia isn't home now and we miss her pretty bad
but she'll be home for Christmas and then we'll all be glad.
Seay plays basketball and hockey, and so does Mark his brother
and when they have some time to spare, they beat up on each other!

Walt and I play cribbage, and I always take a beating.
It can't be that I'm really dumb; it must be 'cause he's cheating!
So now it's nearly Christmas and there's lots of things to do.
There's shopping, cleaning, baking and some decorating too.

My gosh, it's getting late, we still have to trim the tree!
So here's hoping that your Christmas is as HAPPY as can be!

To Lake Erie's Shores, Kingsville Ontario

In 1974 Walt was relocated for a new position with his company. By then, Georgia was enrolled in Forestry at the University of Alberta in Edmonton, Alberta, so we were only four making the big move to Kingsville situated on the shores of Lake Erie in southern Ontario.

That year I made another decision that has influenced the past 50 (and counting) years of my life. I joined the Kingsville Golf and Curling Club and there, soon after our arrival, I met my dearest friend Betty. Although I have always loved sports, especially curling, golf and tennis, I enjoyed most success as a curler. I was fortunate to spend many years travelling with Betty to bonspiels and championships all over Ontario. We were part of a mixed curling team that won the Southern Ontario championship. Spending time at the golf course is one of my favorite pastimes. In fact, recently, on my 90th birthday, I golfed there with my sons and grandson!

It was after thirty years of marriage that Walt and I divorced. The marriage breakup was a hard time for all of us. That year, 1983, I got my real estate license and worked in that business until 2007. My friend Betty was my partner in real estate for many years.

Although busy with real estate, travel, friends, family and golf, I began to spend more time writing poetry and stories. I was fortunate to join a wonderful little group of talented writers who encourage and support me in my writing and in life!

Even when very young I loved writing poems and school assignments. At twelve I decided to write a love story, never getting past the first line, "The large black limousine drove slowly down the avenue, pulling into the drive of a huge estate in the Upper West Side." That was it, my novel. Really, my only attempts at fiction have been bedtime stories. My granddaughters suggested characters and I moulded them into stories that were never written down.

When I was about to marry, I was approached by the editor of the Stettler Independent newspaper. He wanted me to write a column telling about my life moving about Alberta in a mobile home with my oil exploring husband. I was excited but, when Walt heard about it, he didn't approve, so I let it be. I think I have always regretted that decision.

Throughout my life I have celebrated friends and family with poetic tributes and enjoyed writing for special occasions and gatherings. My stories, sometimes based on memories, are always written because I have been inspired by life's little incidents. I stop and notice these moments, they intrigue me and soon become one of my stories. Over the years I have met a lot of interesting characters, so hopefully these people pop up once or twice in my stories!

I feel life has been very good to me, blessing me with great parents, children and siblings. A host of wonderful friends grace my life, many are more like family. I have had good health, plenty of interests and activities to enjoy and opportunities to travel but I always love coming home!

Even though I have vivid memories of my prairie roots, Kingsville and its people hold a special place in my heart. Having lived here nearly fifty years already, I well and truly call it home.

Conflicts in Love

I don't think it's possible to have a relationship without some conflict. It is life, from wars fought all over the planet to our petty little disagreements. Over the years I have given a great deal of thought to conflict within love relationships.

When anger rears its ugly head, it does untold damage. Why? Because most of us are just inarticulate. We are very human beings at our best and in anger our weaknesses become more pronounced. (True, if we always keep our feelings buried, a good shot of anger may allow us to express emotions we didn't know existed.)

The problem with anger and conflict within a love relationship is our inability to separate wheat from chaff when the angry moment passes. Can we wipe from our thoughts words and actions that resulted only in the heat of the moment? And then can we take meaningful parts to heart and work with them?

Often the words "never" and "always" are used to extreme in angry accusations. The accuser seldom means those words literally but uses them to emphasize or exaggerate a point. But on the receiving end, lacking a good defensive retort, one focuses on "never" or "always." This can create a scar that takes much longer to heal.

What really counts at times like this is the ability to step back and understand the importance of this person in your life. And also to accept that the original problem may never be completely resolved. Yes, it may be softened or changed for a while, but in the future, in all likelihood, it could cause yet another battle royal.

It's crucial to be able to remember the feelings that originally attracted us to the one we love. And, if possible, we can try to recreate those emotions to form a stronger, more lasting love and mutual respect.

Real lasting love shouldn't need ropes, physical or emotional, to keep it strong. From time to time we require breathing space so we can return with renewed vigor and a resolve to hang in there. Love doesn't give up but I think sometimes it rests. Sometimes it just goes away for some "R and R."

I guess this is why, in a marriage, a solid friendship is such a good start, not platonic, but loving and supportive. To actually enjoy the company of that important person day in and day out is rare to impossible. There has to be time to seek out the company of friends or just feel comfortable in our own solitude. This is an important mix that usually serves to make a return to love much sweeter.

No one has the perfect answer. Life and love are part of a constant journey toward an elusive goal often just out of our grasp. A great deal of joy can be found in that journey. But some, the lucky ones, manage to brush that goal again and again and nearly always stay within a heartbeat.

God knows that I'm not perfect and now you know it too.
Please look at me more with your heart than other people do.
Know that your face is in my mind, your presence ever dear.
I only seek adventures to fill your patient ear.
My selfish pleasures please forgive, a fault I can't deny.
In honesty, they'll still persist though I will always try.
But when I stumble in your eyes, and angry words are uttered,
my heart's beat has not really stopped but, yes, perhaps it fluttered.

Meeting Betty 1974

October it was, in '74, the curling club the place.
The meeting was over and there you were
with a smile upon your face.
"You're new," you said, "I'm Betty."
And a great friendship began.
The bond, we were both curlers,
and from Saskatchewan.

How grateful I have always been
for that day and that meeting
especially when I felt quite lost
until that friendly greeting.
We shared a drink, no, not a tea,
though there'd be lots of those.
And the number shared throughout the years?
The count just grows and grows.

Someday I'm going to make a list
and, my, will it be full,
of all the places we have been
and never was it dull.
We're older now and slower, yes,
but the good times just don't end.
I look forward to every day
that I have you, my friend.

Joan Harder

Joan and Betty, Mixed Curling Champions Southern Ontario

Hospital Waiting Room

Nothing to keep me from looking around.
Telephones, footsteps and yawns,
voices echo through the halls.
Stretchers, wheels bumping along.
Worried faces strive for calm.
Youngsters, grandmas, no age class is spared.
In the hospital waiting room
No stereo filters through the air.
There's no music to be sick by.
No superficial jollity
can change what we are here for.
No friends nor family's best intentions
can rid the thing they fear for.
No trumpets sound to show the world
these heroes on parade.
And only God knows of what valor
the brave ones are made.

So when you feel that life has dealt you
less than a fair hand…
perhaps an hour of waiting room
will greatly change your stand.

Joan Harder

Friends in Tough Times

You've stood beside me all these years
through thick and sometimes thin
and there've been tears and sadness
but more often there's a grin!

So, on the days when smiles get lost
and joy just can't be found
remember that this too shall pass
and happiness abound.

If I could take your sadness
and throw it far away
I'd order tons of happy times
to come to you and STAY.

But life seems full of curves and twists
to keep us on our toes.
It's up to you and me, I guess,
to make each weed a rose.

So let's both try to see the joy
that really does abound.
It's hidden round the corners
but with faith it can be found!

The Scoop on Soup

On a cold day when snow squeaked under my boots on my way home from school, the scent of homemade soup wafting through the house was the next best thing to heaven. *I wonder, is there soup in heaven? I certainly hope so.* Over the years I have tried hard to create that little bit of heaven on earth in a soup pot.

My friend Betty and I always have shared a love of homemade soup, agreeing that few soups can be recreated the same way over and over again. Betty's mother was an expert in the soup making field. When Baba visited we enjoyed many a bowl. Each batch was delicious, but slightly tweaked in flavor.

So saying, yesterday we decided to make soup for supper. We were spending a day together watching curling and chose a simple cream of potato chowder. I took a small saucepan from the cupboard, put a small amount of salted water in it and set it on the stove to make vegetable stock. Betty said she had chicken broth at home, so she went to get it. I dumped out the water, heated the chicken stock instead. Betty volunteered to dice a large potato and onion. She added it to the simmering broth. Rummaging through the vegetable drawer I discovered a sad looking broccoli floweret and a carrot. I chopped them and added both to the pot, for color, I explained.

Now the pot was full and we had yet to add milk. Back into the cupboard for a larger pot into which we poured our concoction. It had taken on a greenish hue. Salt, pepper, garlic, Montreal steak spices were added, tasted and added again until we agreed on the flavor. For good luck I threw in a large piece of butter. Simmering continued. Betty stirred while I added heated milk and a generous slosh of cereal cream for good measure. At this point it occurred to me I always added niblet corn to potato soup, so in went half a cup. Now the vegetables were tender and tasting began again in earnest. Betty suggested mashing the vegetables to thicken the broth, a good idea. We added a bit of cream of mushroom soup as thickening to make it hearty. This accomplished, we tasted and tested and stirred as the finished product bubbled gently.

A few crackers and some bread sticks made our meal complete. As usual we said we would never be able to make that soup the same way again!

Memories of London (watching William and Kate's wedding)

Well, we were not in London for the royal affair, but I did look forward to seeing some of the familiar sights I remembered from 1990 when my buddy Betty and I took a trip to Europe.

After arriving at London Heathrow Airport, we boarded a double decker bus to take us to the Barbasin Hotel where we were to meet our tour group. We informed our bus driver of our destination and he said he would give us plenty of warning so we wouldn't miss our stop. Being green tourists, we wanted to see all we could so we climbed to the top deck of the bus, and pushed our way to the front. No one was going to interfere with our view of London. Full of excitement we took our seats and waited to begin our adventure.

Off went our bus. Immediately we found ourselves breathing in a cloud of smoke from a diesel stack that blew directly into our faces. Now we knew why no one got upset when we pushed to the front! Nevertheless, we were in London on a double decker bus and we were going to enjoy it come hell, high water or smoke fumes!

During the ride we struck up a conversation with a fellow rider who was quite knowledgeable about this indescribably large city. She knew our hotel, so we relaxed, put our feet up on the front rail, coughed a bit in the fumes and enjoyed the ride. After what seemed a very long time, not boring, but long, our companion said we should go down and get our bags as we were approaching our stop. We rushed down stairs to the baggage compartment. As the bus came to a stop, Betty jumped off on the sidewalk while I threw our bags off the bus.

Just as I leapt to the street the bus driver yelled in a cockney accent, "Not 'ere, oil tell ya when yer stop comes up! 'Op back on and 'urry!" I jumped back on the bus while Betty proceeded to throw our several bags onboard. There was no doubt we were tourists. Red faced with embarrassment we heard the poorly disguised laughter of seasoned riders. But we did arrive safely at our hotel.

For the next ten days we travelled Europe with wonderful people from all over the world: two Australian housewives, a retired couple from Brazil, an 80 year old lady from California, a couple from New York, two Texan couples (who, incidentally, were impressed by absolutely nothing) and a smattering of Canadians. Most delightful of all were two couples from Wales on a joint honeymoon. Why? Because they didn't want to travel alone! We shared hilarious times with the honeymooners as nothing ever seemed to go according to plan. There was a lovely young man from Montreal who spoke six languages and wanted to accompany Betty and me wherever we went because he said we weren't boring. He was 6 feet tall and we felt safe with him. But those are stories for another time.

On our return to London we had several days on our own. We took advantage of the opportunity to see *The Phantom of the Opera* at Queen Elizabeth Theatre and also Agatha Christie's *The Mousetrap*. We toured St. Paul's Cathedral, went to evensong at the Abbey and had tea at Windsor Castle.

Since it was the week before Queen Elizabeth's birthday, we sat on Victoria's statue in front of Buckingham Palace and watched a rehearsal of the full dress parade in her honor. In the actual parade the Queen was to ride in the carriage. Today it was her daughter Princess Anne who waved to us and Prince Charles accompanied her on horseback. It was a magnificent sight. Hundreds of mounted guards, beautiful prancing horses, colorfully uniformed bands marched in perfect order. All passed in a parade that seemed to go on forever. What a memory!

I can only guess the excitement of today's onlookers at the once in a lifetime event.

The Wedding Dress

My daughter Georgia has never ceased to surprise and delight me, but over the years some of the surprises have been preempted by shock and dismay.

When Georgia and Stan decided to tie the knot after seven years together, I happened to be in Hawaii with my mom, Ruby. It was late February when we got a call with the news. The wedding date was a short two months away. Feeling no need for a long engagement, Georgia and Stan planned a small ceremony with a few close friends and relatives. As Georgia explained, "It's really a formality, no big deal, we have been together for years!"

Georgia's brother and his wife had already booked a trip for that time and begged Georgia to change her plans so they could be there. But Georgia explained, "We're farmers, we have to get crops in. Before we know it, it will be haying season and it's really no big deal!" With this we all greatly disagreed. After all this was our Georgia and her brothers wanted to be there, "big deal" or not. Arguments were to no avail, May 5th was written in stone.

Georgia had lived away from home since leaving for the University of Alberta on her 18th birthday. After graduation she was employed with the Alberta government in Grande Prairie. Our visits were rare and precious, but we knew Georgia lived a life she loved. She drove a truck, raised and rode horses and lived on a ranch with a man who shared her passions.

It was decided I would fly to Alberta a few days before the wedding to visit. By this time the wedding had grown to well over a hundred guests.

My plan was complicated by a letter found under my apartment door on my return from Hawaii. My landlord said I had to move by the end of April. My friends went into action, scouring the area for apartments I could afford, no small task. About mid-April a colleague announced she had found it. A quick tour and I was sold. Three bedrooms, second floor, private entrance and reasonable rent included cable. Now for the move. Since my divorce I moved a number of times. My youngest son, his friends and mine were tired of my moves. Good sports though! By the end of the month I was ensconced in my new digs. Standing on tiptoe at my kitchen window I could just glimpse the lake!

Georgia and Stan many years later riding in Arizona

May 2nd was the earliest I could get to Grande Prairie. Georgia cheerfully greeted me at the airport. "It's so great to have you Mom. You can help me with a few things I have to do before Saturday." I was so happy to see her I didn't even ask what.

The next morning we had a lovely breakfast. After coffee Georgia disappeared into the bedroom and came out wearing her lovely satin wedding dress with scalloped hem line and sequined bodice. She had sewn the sequins so tastefully. Modelling the dress, Georgia pointed out that, despite the lovely drape of the skirt, the material was sheer and clingy. That was when she explained what the "thing" we had to do was. We needed to line this skirt with its intricate scalloped hemline and Georgia did not have a sewing machine. I guess, in retrospect, it was probably a good thing because it had been several years since I tried my hand at using one and this was a critical operation. I panicked at the prospect of hand sewing the lining into such a full circle of skirt.

Nonplussed by the prospect, Georgia had more faith in me than I deserved. She cheerfully unrolled a large piece of brown paper on the floor, and spread the skirt out on the paper. With a pencil she roughly traced a line around the skirt. Her enthusiasm caught hold, I grabbed a pencil and started on the other side. Eventually we met. It took a bit more brainpower to figure out the waist but, by guess and golly, we got that drawn. Then we cut out the pattern we had made, and sat back with satisfaction. At least we had started.

After more coffee we tackled pinning the paper pattern to the lining. Georgia felt that would take too long, so with scissors we cut around the pattern as neatly as possible. By this time we came to realize that no one but the two of us would ever see the lining. So we basted the waist to the inside of the dress, making sure the lining was a couple of inches shorter than the hem. We surveyed our handiwork. *Rough, yes. Adequate, uh huh.* Now, we contemplated the big job, hand sewing the huge circular hemline.

"But Mom, if we just trim it a little more here and there, it won't ever show, no one will be the wiser." By this time our minds had melded into one, it made perfect sense to me. After all, this was my girl. If she was happy with it, so was I.

We carefully pressed the unfinished product, and stowed it safely in a plastic bag on a hanger. It really did look lovely. We toasted our handiwork with a couple of glasses of wine, giggling over our questionable cleverness.

My mother and sister were to arrive soon and we knew the dress would not pass their inspection. We agreed we would deal with that issue if and when it should arise.

It is amazing what a couple of glasses of wine can do.

Next day the bride to be and her maid of honor left for Grande Prairie where they would prepare for the big day. So, with the dress held carefully on Georgia's knee, they set off in the farm truck with shovels, brooms and hay forks standing proudly in their holders behind the cab. Somehow, it seemed so fitting!

How I love that girl!

Finding Megan

Some years ago Georgia and Stan owned a farm beside the Alaska Highway outside of Valleyview, Alberta. When the highway was being widened, part of their land was expropriated giving them an opportunity to buy another farm they had long admired. It had an indoor riding arena, something they'd always wanted.

Getting settled in their new place meant taking away a lot of trash, so they made numerous trips to the local sanitary landfill. On one of these excursions they met a couple who had also recently moved to a nearby acreage, the fellow was a dentist in Valleyview. Conversation turned to Georgia and Stan's new farm and riding arena. Their new acquaintances, it turned out, had a teenage daughter who absolutely loved horses but they had never lived anywhere they could own one. Georgia and Stan proposed that they bring their daughter, Megan, to visit. Perhaps she could learn to ride one of their horses.

From the first time Megan arrived the love affair began. For Megan, it was a love of beautiful horses and the opportunity to learn to ride. For Georgia, and later Stan, it was a chance to enjoy the company of a delightful teenager who was only too happy to spend time riding, playing with the dogs and helping with any job she could do. She quickly wormed her way into their hearts and home, baking cookies, painting barns and becoming a most welcome part of their family.

One day Stan came home from an auction with an orphaned calf that would not eat. Megan was upset about it, and decided to come over every day to hand feed the calf with a baby bottle. With her care, the calf began to thrive. But knowing that the calf's future would eventually be the local abattoir was more than Megan could bear. She asked Stan if she could buy the calf. He determined a fair price, a "toonie" and the deal was made. With this came the calf's name, Toonie. He was moved to Megan's home where her dad and Stan built a fenced area. Each morning before school Megan could be seen leading Toonie on his daily walk. Toonie grew very large, very quickly, and finally a tearful Megan agreed to sell Toonie back to Stan. He was quietly taken off to auction with the other spring calves.

Eventually Megan bought her own horse and, with Stan's help with training, broke it to ride. Megan, guided and supported by Georgia, became a very proficient horsewoman and the two spent many summer days travelling to local horse shows and jumping events.

Megan's life became truly intertwined with those of her parents, their families and Georgia and Stan. All were part of Megan's major life events. High school graduation was a very big day and then there was pride mixed with sadness as Megan left to attend University of Alberta. She followed in her dad's footsteps in Dentistry. Still, summers away from university were spent working in her dad's Valleyview office so Megan continued to visit Georgia and Stan and rode her favorite horse.

But, time marches on and soon Megan's horse had to share her owner's time with a young man who had gained her attention. Many years later, Georgia and Stan continued to be close with Megan and her family, watching this young woman as she grew and moved on to forge a marriage, a family of her own, and a career and working life.

To this day, with a tear in her eye, Georgia still expresses gratitude to Megan's family for so generously sharing their daughter. She and Stan look back fondly to that special day when they, "found Megan at the dump!"

My House (1991)

The picture in the paper was nondescript, a black and white 2" X 2" photo in the local real estate paper. Hard to tell much about it, though obviously it had seen better days, but the glowing ad copy was enough, it convinced me to take a look. Armed with a confirmation from the listing realtor my friend and I approached the place.

In the cruel light of day, it was, as I had feared, much worse than the photo indicated. The front steps were broken down and the porch roof hung at a perilous angle, loosely attached to the house. But those things could be fixed, couldn't they?

On the side of the house we saw another porch or veranda with concrete steps, a solid railing and roof. True, the battered green eaves troughs dangled by a few hangers having long since fulfilled their usefulness. But hey, they could be replaced, couldn't they? We mounted the concrete steps and stopped, stunned. I instinctively reached for what I thought would be a door knob before realizing there was no door, nor was there a door anywhere else on that veranda. Instead, I saw a nice window where I assumed the door had been. Okay, that can be dealt with too, couldn't it?

Now we moved to the back of the house. It was an even bigger disappointment. A crumbling cement block wall partially protected an open concrete stairway to the basement. Those stairs were next to what was once a back stoop (okay an old word, but it suited). This too was crumbling, and led to a back door. To the right, attached to the house was, maybe a shed? No stairway to the house, so a leap was needed to access the door. But hey, that could be remedied too, couldn't it?

By now I began to have doubts about even going inside. But my friend and real estate partner Betty, always the optimist, insisted. So we went back to the shaky front porch, climbed the rickety steps and opened the door. We were surprised to find a completely up to date kitchen inside the front door, odd in an older home. Further in was a large dining room and, at the back of the house, a cozy living room and stairway to the second floor.

I opened a door at the bottom of the stairs expecting the worst, as it pretty well had to be the bathroom. Then and there I was smitten. It was a bathroom, but like nothing we expected in an old house. It was so spacious, with walls and ceiling of cedar, forest green tiled floors, a separate shower and a delightful old fashioned tub with room to stretch. Behind me, Betty had a similar reaction.

We finished the tour noting missing light fixtures and closet doors. I thought the loft room upstairs would make a perfect master bedroom. *Secretly I wondered if it was called a master when occupied by a Ms?*

Betty, acting as my realtor, was excited about the house but we agreed not to make an offer until my son had seen it. A lot of work had to be done to make the exterior presentable and my finances and ability were limited. However, the moment my son toured the house his reaction was, "Mom, offer them full up and I'll get to work on the outside right away." So with that promise, and my friendly realtor waiving commission to make up for my chintzy offer, the deal was made.

Joan's House

The day of closing came. The top stair to my very own bedroom became a special spot that day. Ever since my divorce seven years and five different rentals ago, I dreamed of someday owning my own home again. As we sat together on that top step, no one felt happier for me than my friend Betty.

Perhaps there should have been champagne to celebrate the occasion, but the only liquids flowing that day were tears of joy.

Fear

It is such a little word. It doesn't really depict the emotion, but adding an adjective can bring it closer to the dread or foreboding we feel. Most of us can describe something that causes a cold fist-like clout to our solar plexus. Fear can take on the persona of a fierce enemy. Well, it is our enemy, it has the power to send us cowering in corners of our minds where we quickly slam doors shut.

I recognize (in saner moments) that my fears are relatively small. Or they would be if they were another person's. In that case, I could show superb wisdom, figuring out ways to conquer anxiety and put fears to rest. But alone in my room in the middle of the dark night those assuring words easily thrown out to others are impossible to conjure for my own comfort. Then, no matter how cozy I am under my warm quilt, those noiseless but real doubts start tip toeing up the stairs. So real that I cover my head, worried that if I dare to open my eyes they will take shape.

Will I be able to pay my bills at the end of the month? Do I owe money, have I forgotten to repay? Do my kids know how very much I love and appreciate them? And conversely can I be sure they still love and appreciate me? Do I do enough for charity? Am I truly a good and honorable friend? Will I ever sell another house? Does my sister really forgive me for the terrible haircut I gave her when she was six? *Something tells me Mom probably didn't but it's too late for that.*

Will I wake up one morning as a prisoner in my own body? That is my great phobia, the "claustro" one. I test myself, body rigid, eyes wide open, imagining my only communication is with my eyes. When I close my eyes tightly, thinking what would it be like to never see again, that fist really packs a wallop. But I have no answer, I just self-inflict more misery. If I become ill or disabled will I have strength of character to deal with it? Could I support loved ones if this befalls them? As I huddle under the covers no answer is forthcoming. Thoughts course in quick succession until, at last, I admit these fears are not the kind I can resolve, even in the comforting light of day. I rely on my personal solution. I pray, silently passing the buck into the hands of a far more capable being. Then I uncover my eyes and look bravely around the shadowy room.

Just before I drift to sleep I know that, just like Scarlet O'Hara, I'll think about it tomorrow.

To Do or Not to Do, That Is the Question

I am drowning in a sea of "to do" lists. I always rely on lists to try to keep myself focused. Unfortunately, lists are often misplaced or ignored. However, since retiring at the end of July, I am beginning to think that, with all my new found free time, I may actually start taking those lists seriously and accomplish wonderful things.

At the top of my list is organizing my writing and hopefully doing a lot more. Then of course, there are the dozens of jobs that are always there and easy to ignore; cleaning out closets and drawers (*yawn*), and going through the filing cabinet to shred unnecessary outdated contracts and warranties on things I no longer have. Purging service records and bills for cars that long ago passed on sounds like a good idea too. And so does completely rearranging my back porch to discover just where my tools are. Speaking of tools, I want to make a plan to start using them again on some favorite woodworking projects. The list goes on and on.

In reality, none of the things on my list seem to happen. Instead, nice days are spent on the golf course pursuing my favorite (albeit frustrating) sport in the vain hope of actually improving. This after some fifty odd years of playing the game with little flash of genius. *At 76, I don't like to think it but maybe that ship has sailed.*

Except for the everyday "must dos" that go along with owning a home with a large yard, I am not crossing anything off on my list. Instead new things crop up: mice in my kitchen, ants in cupboards and the worst and most expensive issue, grubs in my lawn. The mouse is a goner, the ants are discouraged and the grubs? They are facing slow elimination, I hope, by killer stuff, over seeding and spreading four yards of #1 topsoil over the lawn. This with the help of my friend

Joe. With a kind rain shower now and the promise of warmer, good germinating weather next week, I watch for the first sign of healthy little green fuzz to appear.

In the meantime, I am back to making more lists. Ho hum.

Joan Harder

Autumn Leaves and Other Jobs

October, wow, how time does fly!
Summer's gone in the blink of an eye.
The trees were green just yesterday
but leaves are dropping every day.
I check my list of things to do.
I made it in June, but I've checked off so few.
I must wash the windows one of these days,
I'm tired of looking outside through a haze.
There's a basket of ironing that cries for attention,
and the cobwebs are really too many to mention.
There's food in the back of the fridge that's been there
for so long that the cottage cheese probably has hair.
I won't use the oven 'cause I can't stand the smoke.
I'm right out of Easy Off, really, that's no joke.
The shed door was desperately in need of paint.
My visiting daughter did that, she's a saint.
The fertilizer's ready to energize my lawn.
I bought it last year, just didn't put it on!
Now I'm really quite sure that these jobs will get done.
It's not that I'm lazy, I'm just having fun.
So when golfing is over, and my card friends go south
I'll get busy and never be down in the mouth.
And if I'm very lucky, I'll still have writer friends
and I'll work very hard at making amends.

Florida, Here We Come (March 9, 1993)

We're wheelin' down I 75
feelin' glad to be alive.
Sure, it's ten thirty on a Tuesday morn
and we're blessin' the day that we were born.

I woke up this mornin' at 5:32
even before the cock had crew (?)
Got the suitcase out and packed it
threw in the clubs and tennis racket.

The wagon was full and rarin' to go.
We left the little red bomb for Joe!
Stopped at the tunnel to buy some booze,
headed south and set the cruise.

The snow is disappearin'
there's nothin' here but grass.
You ask if we're happy?
You bet your sweet ass!

Just passed Dayton and goin' strong.
Sure hope we stop to eat 'fore long.
Think I'll have pancakes and jelly
and maybe some bacon for my little belly.

All last week I shovelled snow,
lookin' forward to the day we'd go
south to warm and salt sea air,
expose those legs, so white and bare!

Dar and Michelle don't ever talk
lost in their walkman world of rock
while here in front, one drives, one nods.
It's Streisand tapes for us old broads.

Joan Harder

We left I 75 and took
I 71 in the trip tik book.
Through Cincinnati and a traffic jam
I was cool, but Betty said, "Damn!"

From there we headed for Kentucky,
blue grass, derby and "horse-pucky."
We cut through hills of solid rock.
Betty's at the wheel, what a jock!

Headin' for Nashville, wheels a-hummin'
can't wait to hear those "geetars" strummin'.
Betty's driving gives us the yips
what with tappin' her toes and swingin' her hips.

We've got the jump, or so to speak,
next week spring break will hit its peak.
Thousands of scholars escapin' their schools,
off to the beaches where there ain't no rules!

Out of sight of watchful eyes,
Comin' home burned and tellin' lies!
Some of them happy…lots of fun,
others not sure what all they done!

The Last Time I Saw My Mother

She was celebrating her 80th birthday and we had all gathered at my sister's home for a big party. Invitations had been sent far and wide. Ruby had many friends and was loved by all.

It was my Aunty Ruby, who as a young woman, gave up her job to care for her sister, our Mom and then stayed on to care for us. Later when she and my dad were married she was still Aunty Ruby to us, but eventually we dropped "Aunty" and called her Ruby. Over time our little family changed with the births of Barb and baby brother John. By this time, with Dave finishing high school, I was babysitter of choice, much to my chagrin. Oh, I loved those little duffers but after all I was growing up, or so I thought.

Our family had increased by one more person, my Papa. We moved to a bigger house and somehow our mixed up group managed to coexist quite happily under one roof. Well, okay, maybe not always happily. Papa was a cantankerous old Welshman in his 70s and Dad expected everyone, including Ruby, to defer to Papa at all times. That wasn't always easy.

More years passed. Dave and I married and moved away and Papa died. Finally, after eleven years, Ruby had a reasonably normal household that included just herself, Dad and their two kids. We always stayed close as a family and spent many holidays together, never thinking of Ruby as anyone but our mother. She was patient, kind and loving and a wonderful homemaker and caregiver.

Ruby and Cliff

On my dad's 80th birthday we all gathered in Stettler for a huge party. Dad enjoyed it immensely, revelling in the celebration. He had always loved seeing his whole family together, but at this party he also had a whole town of friends to enjoy on his special day.

Then, just three weeks later, Dad suddenly passed away. This brought us all together once more, this time to support Ruby in her grief and shock. There were so many adjustments for our Ruby. Dad had always taken care of bills, driving, repairing and many family decisions and by this time none of their children lived nearby to help in day to day matters.

Over time Ruby became adept at bus travel to visit her children. She continued to live in her little home keeping close track of a host of family and friends. Somewhere about this time it dawned on me that I no longer called her "Ruby." Unconsciously I had begun saying "Mom." Mom never let on that she noticed, but I've always wondered if she did. It was so natural I can't remember having made the change.

For a while after Dad died, Mom confided that she really didn't like going home to her house anymore, it just meant being terribly lonely. But she was determined to stay and make the best of it. Not too many months after this confession, as I drove her to the airport for her flight home, she smiled and said, "I finally can look forward to my little house again, it just took a while to get used to the empty chair." Tears flooded my eyes and I understood what a journey she had made.

Now, ten years after Dad's death, there she was, perky and laughing, dressed like a beautiful little princess, enjoying being the center of attention at her 80th birthday party. She was happily renewing old acquaintances with friends and relatives. Some had traveled hundreds of miles to pay homage to their beloved Ruby. Her silver hair was tinged a slight blue, as was her style, and a cigarette was in her hand. It was a habit none of us had the heart to try to break. Her smile was what we all loved to see.

It was July 25th, Ruby was named for her birthday gem. It was a wonderful day for all of us.

Thomas Family at Ruby's 80th Birthday Party in Calgary

Four months later, almost to the day, she anticipated a trip to Calgary for the Christmas season, having dutifully made her special plum puddings for the occasion. This time she had attached a copy of her recipe to the lid of each jar. She obviously thought it was time we all made our own.

The next day my brother Dave was to pick her up for the drive. Sadly someone more powerful had a different plan. Our beloved Mom took her last trip November 25th.

I felt honored to be asked to give Mom's eulogy at her funeral. I was proud and I think she was smiling too.

On the way back to the house after the ceremony, my brother-in-law said, "Let's not do 80th birthday parties anymore, okay?"

And we all agreed.

The Dress

Over the years I have gradually changed my style of clothing, partly due to my changing figure (okay, weight gain) and also because I no longer felt the need to be alluring, chic and sexy. Ha! To be honest, those never were high on my list and pretty well unattainable through most of my life.

Anyway, the point is, I never have had many dresses in my closet and each one there was purchased for a specific occasion. I guess they are a sort of sartorial history of my life in the closet (*not that kind of closet!*)

There was Mark and Joanie's wedding in 1986 when I was resplendent in lemon yellow and weighed about 150. In 1988 at the occasion of Seay and Carena's wedding my dress was a bit unusual. For the Hindu ceremony I borrowed a sari from the bride's mother. The next day at the church wedding I was decked out in a pale coral shift with a matching striped over jacket. Very smart I thought. In 1990 came daughter Georgia's marriage to Stan. Wanting to fit the western scene I found a mustard suit decorated with what I liked to think was a lariat motif. Again, very sharp, but perhaps a size larger than the last wedding.

Sadly in 1993 I needed a dress for a somber occasion, the death of my dear Ruby. Since she had always been a bright spot in our family, I chose not to wear traditional black but a subdued green shift with matching floral jacket. She would have approved, I know. As some funerals are, this one, although sad, was also a time of warmth and laughter as we shared our favorite memories of Ruby.

A few years later I was invited to the wedding of a family friend. After happily shedding fifteen pounds, I felt I needed, no, deserved, to shop for a new dress. Styles had changed and ankle length dresses were popular. Off I went to the dress shop. Struggling as I pulled full length heavily brocaded and lined monstrosities over my head, I panicked a couple of times and called for help! I was ready to leave the store empty handed. *What the heck, a nice pant suit would suffice.* But as I left, on a "Reduced for Sale" rack I spied a lovely gold dress with an over jacket, not too heavy, tastefully buttoned and miracle of miracles, it was my size! I asked the clerk why this particular dress was marked down and was told clothing on that rack had small defects. Looking the dress over I found none and decided to take a chance. The dress worked very nicely for that occasion and also for my god child's wedding two years later. Thankfully my weight was on hold. However, I must confess, each time I wore that outfit I carefully examined it, still looking for the defect. I was always nervous that some more observant person would see it and bring it to my attention. When I wore it I always felt I had to sit down or back up against a wall to hide the defect that must have been somewhere in the back.

This past summer we had so much hot humid weather. It was a challenge to find something comfortable to put on my ample figure, again up a few pounds. A friend suggested that long, simple, colorful cotton sundresses were attractive on a variety of figures. Again I began the search only to abandon it after the usual try-ons and shocking visions of myself in unflattering fitting room mirrors.

Then one day, out of the blue, I spied a soft green, straight line dress with a gecko design below the neckline and a moon and star motif applique around the hem. Since I had recently visited Arizona, I was drawn to the southwestern feel of the dress. It was my size and, even more delightful, it was a sidewalk sale, marked down 70%. At first I was suspicious, was this another defective dress? No, the clerk kindly explained. It was marked down because the size was not a good seller.

Uh huh, so I'm the only one in town that wears XL? I swallowed my pride. In the privacy of the fitting room, and despite the mirror, I fell in love!

Fat Folks (1978)

Is it true what they say about fat folks?
Do they pant at the thought of the stairs?
Do they jiggle whenever they giggle?
And look like they're travelling in pairs?

Is a meal their idea of excitement
over anything else that they do?
Do they finish up all the leftovers
long after the "skinnies" are through?

Do they all wear their clothes in "queen" sizes
and bulge at the seams of their jeans?
Look back with nostalgia at photos
of how slick they were in their teens?

If it's true then I don't want to be one!
I'd rather have one chin than two.
I'll walk through my life, and not waddle....
Let the elephants live in the zoo!

I'll say "no thanks" to all second helpings,
and pass up the ice cream and pie.
I'll nibble on carrots and celery,
no peanuts or French fries for I.

Then I'll smile at myself in the mirror
and, when finally I meet with my fate,
I'll know it won't say on my tombstone...
"It must have been something SHE ATE!"

A Week in Myrtle Beach

Doing what we love to do,
tee up a favorite dimpled sphere
in the early morning dew.
Hit that ball and watch it rise
suspended in the cloudless skies.
But first, a moment's reverie
standing on the balcony.
The steaming coffee vapors rise
to meet the sight that greets our eyes.
A burning sun ball slips its bonds
to flood the ocean skies beyond.
While down below, to left and right
we're treated to the peaceful sight
of sun touched surf on unmarked sand
still free from all the young and tanned.

It's much too much the joy I feel.
I pinch myself, "Can this be real?"
And then, the voice of my cart-mate,
"Oh gosh! Too bad that wasn't straight!"

Our Trip West with "The Eagle"

Several years ago Betty and I decided to take a trip west. Since we loved the open road and had many destinations in mind, we decided to drive. The weather was exceptionally hot so we carried a good supply of refreshments in a cooler for rest stops. Betty, the more organized of our twosome, marked maps with our route, stops, and, oh yes, casinos on the way. We packed golf clubs and tennis racquets. As a rule we never have known how to travel light. As long as there was still room we added everything we could ever need.

Our first day we hoped to get to Bemidji, Minnesota, famous for its Paul Bunyan statue, the Mississippi headwaters and a casino. We didn't have time to see it all, we had a schedule to keep. I planned to visit Estevan, our home for 18 years. In Regina we were to split up, I would visit a friend while Betty took the car to her in-laws and mother. I was to go by bus to visit Barb in Calgary. Betty would stop to see cousins and meet me there. A well planned schedule, or so we thought.

We made it to Bemidji, overnighting at a tidy inexpensive motel. The drive was longer than expected, so first things first. I showered while Betty found an ice machine and prepared cocktails from the ever important travel bar. Then we went in search of a good hamburger joint. Bemidji was a typical tourist town, so in no time we found a small friendly bar. We relaxed over cold beer and great food. Later we checked out the oversized Paul Bunyan statue. Yes, he did look like a lumberjack in a black and red checkered shirt, proudly holding a very large axe in his very large hand. Next to him was a very large blue ox. *Uh huh, as advertised.* Early to bed to be ready for the next leg of our trip. Or so we thought.

Saturday We thought the town would be teeming with tourists so we quickly packed our bags in our overloaded car and picked up complimentary coffee as we checked out. We headed west planning to stop later for breakfast. Happily, traffic was light. Highway 2 West was a four lane highway with a wide grassy expanse separating oncoming traffic. We enjoyed the wooded scenery, sipped our coffee and cruised.

Within minutes of the city limits, out of the corner of my eye something flashed in the meridian. Betty yelled and I hit the brakes as we slammed into a deer bounding across the lane. It landed squarely in front of us. The sound was deafening but the deer got on its feet and moved into the trees. We came to a stop on the shoulder as steam poured from the radiator and the motor died. We stared at each other, too stunned to speak. Everything happened in the blink of an eye. It was 10:00am Saturday and our vacation was at a standstill. We examined the damage. Hood, grill, radiator, headlight and fender were toast. At that moment it dawned on us that we were lucky to be okay.

As we pondered our next move an older car pulled up behind us. The driver, a man about fifty, got out. He wore a shirt, jeans and a felt hat and sported a neat grey mustache. He asked if we had trouble. We pointed to our car, antifreeze now pooled on the pavement. When we told him about the deer, he said, not to worry, this was a reservation and he was sure venison would be on the menu today. He was most concerned to help and, really, he was our only option. He offered to take one of us ahead to make a call to CAA saying that with all our luggage, we shouldn't both leave. While we thought this over, he went to his car and returned with a business card with his photo identifying him as a private investigator. He said he was on his way home after participating in a drug bust. At this point we decided to take his offer. Betty stayed in the car, doors locked, and I joined our rescuer.

We drove to a small service station where we asked for the phone. The guy behind the counter wanted a dollar for the call and our helper quickly paid. CAA told me that a flatbed truck would arrive in half an hour.

Our private eye drove me back to the car where Betty and our belongings were secure. Before he left I asked if he carried a gun. Yes, but he'd only used it once. *Don't know why I needed to know.* He waved off our offer of money for gas saying he was glad to help. We flooded him with thanks and the road service truck arrived. Although it didn't quite fit the situation, I was reminded of Lone Ranger stories of my youth. As our helper drove away, I said to Betty, "And we don't even know his name." This was just the beginning of our unexpected week in Bemidji, Minnesota.

Our car loaded, we climbed in the cab with the driver. On our way to the garage in Bemidji, our driver warned us it was closed on Saturdays. We had to wait until Monday to contact the owner. Our hearts sank as we thought of all we had to do in the meantime: call about our insurance, find a place to stay for who knows how long, rent a car and tell relatives of our unexpected turn of events. And we didn't even know if the car could be repaired.

In no time we arrived at a well-kept auto repair shop. Seeing movement inside, we looked at each other in disbelief. Someone was taking care of business after all. It turned out that the owner was catching up on books. Sympathetic to our story, he immediately put the car on the hoist and phoned suppliers for parts. He even found the last available rental car in town and arranged immediate delivery so we could unload our baggage. And then he suggested good motels.

The rental car was small but with persistence we managed to transfer all our stuff. As we started our search for a motel, we drove by the local sheriff's office. Perhaps we needed to report the accident, after all, an injured animal was out there. A bored constable assured us it would be taken care of and we left.

We drove by two motels before settling on a Best Western. Approaching the front desk I let Betty do the talking. The friendly woman at the desk said they had a second floor room available, a double overlooking the pool. It sounded perfect, but my heart sank because we didn't know how much it would be.

Well, the clerk said, "It's $75.00 a night." Before I had a chance to say a thing, Betty turned and walked away. The clerk was a bit surprised. So was I! I couldn't believe my ears when to Betty's retreating back the clerk said, "Well, what would you want to pay?"

That's when my pal went into action. Instead of replying, she told the long sad story of our tragic deer incident, ruined trip, worried families, wrecked car and finished the saga saying we had no idea how long our stay might be. We hoped for something around 40 or 50 dollars.

By this time the clerk was totally involved, "So $50.00 a night would be okay?"

I hardly waited to get out of there before flinging my arms around the best little negotiator ever! We laughed giddily as we unloaded our baggage and wheeled it to the elevator. In the room, first of all we unpacked our travelling bar. I went for ice while Betty called her mother to tell her of our delay. Her God fearing Catholic Baba's immediate reaction, in a mixture of Ukrainian and English, was to tell Betty to get down on her knees and thank God we weren't killed. Believe me, she was right. Though we didn't get on our knees, we were very thankful. Betty's Baba had a way of getting right to the issue and I loved her for it. What we did do was pour two very healthy whiskies before making another move. Baba would have agreed with that too.

We replayed the day's events, thinking of all the nice people who had a part in making our day better. We decided to pour another before looking over the rest of what would be our home for who knew how long.

The pool area was large and open with second floor balconies above. As we wandered we found a nice restaurant on the main floor. Now I didn't know if it was two whiskies or sudden relaxation after a hectic day, but I felt light headed. That's when it hit me. We hadn't eaten since the night before. We immediately found a table in the dining room for a much needed meal and after eating our fill, we thought of making it an early night. But no, a lovely pool just waited for us, there wasn't a soul there. With towels in one hand and nightcaps in the other, we went to the pool. It was lovely. The cares of the day melted away in the lovely heat of the hot tub and soothing warmth of whiskey. Life was good!

Sunday We woke refreshed, ready to take on whatever awaited us. But it was Sunday and to my friend that meant Mass. After coffee and toast we asked for directions to a Catholic church. I opted to stay while Betty went to church, feeling a touch guilty, but I assured Betty I would be properly pious, maybe even reading the Gideon Bible from the dresser drawer. There was no doubt we had a lot to be grateful for.

That afternoon we tried out a nearby tennis court. Because it was hot for early June and we weren't used to it, our tennis was not vigorous. In the end we felt perhaps a nice cool bar would be better and we found a busy one in town. People were friendly and curious, so we chatted and of course told them of our misfortune. *I must admit it was becoming less unfortunate all the time.* Not knowing how long we would be in town, we heard about a local theatre opening of *Men in Plaid*. We filed this for later discussion.

We drove around town and discovered Bemidji Country Club, a beautiful layout with trees, hills, water and a lovely clubhouse. Greeted by the head pro we learned that the club was semi-private, non-members could play late in the day. Of course, Betty mentioned our predicament and that we were members of a nice club in Canada. The pro welcomed us to come by around 4 pm. If a tee time was available we could play as many holes as daylight allowed. For a twilight rate! Things looked brighter all the time.

Later we returned to our motel to phone family and friends. Monday we hoped to find out how long repairs would take. I thought to myself that my insurance company would want to know about the costs involved. It crossed my mind that if repair was too high they might write off my car, leaving us with a bigger problem. Betty thought that was negative thinking, we should wait and see. She was right, of course. After our calls we continued with what was quickly becoming our evening ritual, cocktails at the pool. Again we were alone, all was quiet. It was Sunday night so the weekenders had probably left. We were getting used to our private luxury.

Monday After a great sleep we visited the garage. The owner spoke to our insurance agent and we were relieved to hear that since we were far from home it was preferable to repair rather than to write off my car. On Friday the work would be completed.

It seemed time to expand our tour so we set off for the head-waters of the mighty Mississippi. Curiously, there was also a casino nearby. Somehow, "headwaters of the Mississippi" had more power in my mind than the reality, a lazy wandering waterway.

Following our map to the nearby casino, we happily changed dollars for rolls of coins, and decided to split up and meet again in an hour. We wished each other luck, and set off to make our fortunes. Up to this point our togetherness had meshed so well. I was amazed that our friendship was bearing up so well through everything. Looking back, even that the thought presented itself to me should have been a warning.

I fed coins into a slot machine, hearing an occasional happy jingle of a win, when there was a tap on my shoulder. Betty had run out of nickels. Because we had been partners in many ventures for years, our finances went back and forth with ease, so handing over rolls of nickels was nothing. Betty left with them in hand.

In a matter of minutes she was back and said, "Well that didn't last long."

I exclaimed, "You have to be kidding!" and roughly handed her another roll of coins. I should have known better. Her reaction was immediate, as was my regret. She hurled the roll back at me and, of course, I did not catch it. It hit the marble tile, splitting and sending coins in all directions. There we were, in the midst of a crowd of onlookers, red faced, scrambling around the floor as nickels rolled everywhere. We glared at each other and left the rest of the scattered coins. With as much dignity as we could manage we exited the building.

The drive back was quiet. I'm not sure who broke the silence, but in no time we were both laughing at our ridiculous behavior, over, of all things, a two dollar roll of nickels. If that was all we could fight about, our friendship was secure. We went golfing and any leftover frustration disappeared as we smacked those little white dimpled balls. The day ended happily with our evening entertainment at the hot tub.

Tuesday We were getting used to the easy going lifestyle we had adopted. After a leisurely breakfast we phoned loved ones who, we assumed, anxiously awaited our arrival and worried about our welfare. By now, though, we shared a guilty suspicion that the deer was the only unfortunate. We were having ourselves a very good time although we told people we were simply doing the best we could in a difficult situation. *Maybe we were a bit too convincing, I sensed empathy fading with each call.*

After an hour working up a sweat at the tennis court, as much from chasing errant balls as from any actual tennis, we headed back to our motel pool. On this, our first daytime visit, we were disappointed to find it busy. After a quick dip, we returned to our room, poured drinks and hauled chairs to our balcony to watch the activity below. Yes, life was good.

We decided to dine in the motel restaurant. Our insurance agent suggested it would make it easier to keep track of expenses and we were happy with that. A nice glass of wine with dinner did a lot to convince Betty the day was over and I too had found myself catnapping. It was still early, the pool was busy and we called it a day. After all, there was always tomorrow.

Wednesday On another glorious sunny morning we discussed the day's possibilities over coffee. It was too hot for tennis and cheap rates at the golf course started later. There was the casino but after due consideration we agreed it was foolhardy to put our friendship in jeopardy again, especially so far from home. Aha, Betty remembered the play and we thought it could be fun, so *Men in Plaid* it was. We spent the day picking up souvenirs, had lunch, of course, and made a trip to the body shop where the Eagle was undergoing a facelift. The shop owner confirmed all would be ready Saturday morning. Two more days of livin' the life. Off we went to get ready for an evening at the "theatah!"

We got directions, had a quick snack, and changed into the best outfits we could, given our trip was planned around golf, tennis, and Georgia's ranch. We hoped clean and neat would suffice at what, apparently, was one of the social events of the summer.

We found the theatre and parked a short walk away. Fortunately, the sun was low so we avoided our customary search for shade, an obsession of Betty's that often required several circuits of a parking lot in order to find the best tree.

The theater lobby was humming. We suspected tickets might be at a premium so we got in line quickly. As we reached the counter we were asked if we had reservations. "No, I'm afraid we're just in town for a couple of days."

The lady behind the counter was surprised. She explained opening night was sold out, perhaps if we came back later? We looked at each other. Again my buddy Betty related our sad tale. We must have appeared pathetic. The nice lady, genuinely concerned, turned to her partner behind the counter asking, "Do you really think the Johnsons will be coming?" Her colleague seemed to read her mind, opened a drawer and handed over an envelope neatly titled JOHNSON. Our gratitude overflowed as we paid for the tickets.

We followed a waiting usher through a large packed theater. We were astonished to find the Johnsons had good seats, fourth row from front. Settling in, yes, we felt a touch guilty, but also we revelled in our good luck. We hoped the Johnsons would get to see the show sometime. The performance was excellent, the music great. Our seats were amazing.

155

We returned to our room later that night, and seeing no one at the pool, opted for our nightly dip and cocktail. We were still amazed at our streak of good fortune.

Thursday After a late night I was happy to stay in bed. Laying there, I thought about our week, a little sad it was coming to a close. The Eagle was going to be ready to fly tomorrow, so we could restart our trip a full week after our collision with the deer. But we still had today. Tomorrow we would transfer our belongings and return the rental car. Over breakfast I would discuss this with my buddy, who I may have mentioned, is the more organized of our twosome. Over the years, I have noticed that my plans often have flaws which Betty seems able to ascertain. We still had a day to do whatever we had missed. "Living the dream" had become a reality for us of late.

Okay, showered and refreshed, we found our favorite table in the restaurant and our smiling waitress brought coffee. By now, we were regulars, very much at home. Betty decided on her favorite eggs Benedict. I chose old English fry-up, an item not usually on an American menu. But having been a *Coronation Street* junkie from way back, I clarified my order as bacon, eggs, hash browns and fried tomatoes. Over coffee we happily discussed ideas for our day. These jelled nicely except for laundry, which Betty felt should be our first endeavour. *It hadn't even occurred to me.*

Laundry was something I did, but to Betty laundry was art. This I learned as a newly single person, when she kindly offered, "Just drop off your laundry, I will do it with mine, no problem." Believe me, I was quick to take that offer! So, that is how I came to spend laundry days watching and learning the fine art of stain treatment and proper folding. I even improved my ironing, a job I hate to this day. All this from a person nine years my junior! To think I fluffed through thirty years of family laundry completely unaware of the RIGHT way.

We found a laundromat and Betty ran in to see if we could get a machine. Apparently Friday was not a big laundry day, the sole person there sat with a book and cigarette while a colorful load tossed in a nearby dryer. She smiled, waving her cigarette toward a bank of idle machines, "They're all yours, be my guest." In no time we had clean, folded, suitcase ready clothes. One more day before we had to pack up for good.

Back at the motel we informed the clerk of our Saturday departure. The weekend probably meant a new set of holidayers and finally our room would be available at a regular rate. There may have been a little twinge of guilt as I caught Betty's eye but it did not deter us from taking full advantage of another day in the sun. We played golf, enjoyed cold beer on a patio overlooking the course and dined at our motel.

Finally, in our bathing suits, once more armed with towels and cocktails, we soaked in the deserted hot tub. It was after ten but we were ready for an early night, there was nothing better to guarantee a great sleep than a relaxing dip. We would miss that.

Friday I woke earlier than usual. This past week had been idyllic, who would have believed everything would turn out so well? Today promised to be busy making arrangements for the car, phoning family and friends and loading the Eagle with our stuff. The great thing was we still had a holiday ahead of us. I had to smile and woke Betty to share my musings.

It was too early to pick up the Eagle, so after our customary leisurely breakfast and coffee, we organized suitcases and checked that we weren't leaving anything behind. Under beds, in drawers, cabinets and closets, everything was checked by me and double checked by my thorough roommate. After many years travelling the curling circuit together, Betty was well aware of my carelessness. Even though it irritated me at times, I must say, she was usually right.

Back at the auto body shop, final touches were completed on our new air conditioner. The mechanic double checked his work, and invited us to take it for a quick run. Must say, it was nice to get behind the familiar dashboard with lovely cool air emanating from the vents. We waited while the car was vacuumed, washed and waxed to perfection.

Suddenly I was excited, we were actually ready to hit the road. I signed papers, we returned the rental and packed the Eagle to be ready for an early morning.

But not before one more great meal, taking time to enjoy our final dinner in Bemidji. The friendly staff treated us like family and Betty, an extremely generous tipper, made sure they would not forget us too quickly. Readying ourselves for a farewell dip in our private pool, we mixed drinks, duly noting that our well-used bar had become a little lighter. Once again we had the quiet pool to ourselves. I had just put my towel and drink on the pool edge when Betty said, "Look, someone is coming." It was no one we had seen before, a man wearing coveralls with "Security Guard" emblazoned on his pocket.

We smiled as he approached, but he frowned. "Did you folks not see the sign on the door? This area is closed after 10:00 pm each night. It's 10:30, you'll have to leave immediately."

Quickly Betty apologized. We let on that we were newcomers and said we would not break the rule again. Collecting drinks and towels and, with a great attempt at straight faces, we said goodnight. Inside our room we burst out laughing. Lucky for us, he wasn't a very secure security guard. And anyway, our stay was over! We finished our drinks. It was another amazing night at the spa.

Saturday We woke early, anxious to see what the rest of our trip had to offer. We wanted to get on the road and stop later for breakfast. As usual, we discussed who would drive first and I won, so off we went.

It was another gorgeous sunny morning as we happily popped Barbra's latest CD in the player. We drove out of town, not without sentimental waves, and Bemidji disappeared in the rear view mirror. We were really on our way. I breathed a sigh of relief passing the spot where we met the deer. This time it was clear sailing. We cruised, content to let Barbra's rendition of "People" be the only sound, except for a quietly humming motor.

Betty was checking her map when an ear splitting explosion was heard underneath the car, a sound I had heard only once before. I eased my foot off the gas, it let up. I pressed the gas only to hear the deafening noise again. We had just blown the muffler! Our ears rang but we had to get to a town, so I tried to keep our speed up. I intermittently stepped on the gas, causing all hell to break loose, and then eased up. The noise was a bit easier to deal with our windows open. Going down the highway in our own little war zone, we erratically sped up and slowed down. Fellow drivers added to our turmoil with their honking and flashing lights.

Mercifully, we hadn't gone far when Betty excitedly shouted that we were nearing a town. We hoped to see a muffler shop, but the first welcome sign was that of a diner. We parked, thankfully turning off the motor. Maybe someone could tell us where to find the nearest auto repair. On our noisy arrival we were met by a friendly smiling waitress who cheerfully directed us to a muffler shop. We thanked her and said we'd be back for breakfast.

The shop wasn't far and the owner didn't have to guess why we were there, but he did have a car on the hoist and was just starting a repair job. I left it to Betty to explain our trip so far. Without a second thought he said, "Well this job can wait, we'll get you on the road first. Here are the keys to my pickup over there. You gals go for breakfast, come back in an hour. By the way, thank the waitress at the diner, she's a friend of mine."

Again we were astonished. Sometimes it was hard to find words to explain how really great people were, especially when you're in a jam, but we sure planned to work on it. That breakfast was the best in the world. We filled the truck with gas before we returned it and were profuse in our thanks when we picked up the Eagle. Once again the motor purred. Our saviour just smiled, wishing us a safe journey. He was pretty sure that hitting the deer dislodged the exhaust system. It was too bad it hadn't been checked. After all our good luck, I was pleased to pay for repairs. Again, we were on our way. Once more we looked forward to holidays with friends and family.

It seemed fitting, when Betty turned on the radio, that Barbra was still singing "People."

The Wager

The first of May was a red letter day
when I stood on the scale, in the nude,
for a weigh.
The dial just sticks on 176.
Clearly that's too much tonnage,
was I in a fix!
So right then and there, and, it seemed very fair,
you issued a challenge,
a wager, a dare.
Could I give up sweets and all fat loaded eats
'til the date of June 1st, that's a month
WITH NO TREATS!
How I gleefully wiggled, my excess flesh jiggled.
'Twas a lark so to speak.
My inner self giggled.
A whole month to lose just ten pounds, I mused.
I'll do that in a week, without
giving up booze!
The wager was set, the winner would get
a crisp ONE HUNDRED DOLLARS.
A respectable bet.
I'd eat carefully all day, but at night
what the hey?
I deserved some small treat
so I nibbled away.

From Prairie Roots to Lake Erie Shores

My days seemed to fly, and soon on Mom's Day
my bathroom scale waited, alone,
high and dry.
Then in a flash, I thought of the $CASH!
I had seriously wagered. Now
it seemed rather rash!
I ran to the scale, my face turning pale.
Just as I expected, I was doomed.
I would fail!
June 1st drawing near, I quivered with fear.
I checked in the mirror, MY GOD
that's MY REAR!
I started on water and veggies and fruit.
I ate turkey and tuna, and gave up
booze to boot.
THE MOMENT OF TRUTH was coming, forsooth
I stood bare on the scales and longed
for my youth.
For the number that showed between my two big toes
read a big ONE SIX EIGHT.
My despondency grows.
But as bad as it sounds, my courage rebounds
for although I have failed, I have still
LOST eight pounds.

As for you, my friend Bet, I have not one regret.
Spend the dough in good health, I'll lose that
ten pounds yet!

Joan Harder

My First Kiss

This moment though fleeting, remains in my thoughts
as fresh as the day it took place.
I thought that I hid it from anyone's view
but the fact was, it showed on my face.
I had noticed before and my stomach would lurch
with desire that burned like a flame.
I was young and undisciplined, but somehow I knew
I would lose if I fell for this game.

So we flirted, I fled, but returned yet again.
The appeal took me quite by surprise.
I'd been told not to touch, but a look shouldn't hurt.
After all, I could just close my eyes.
But our closeness was more than my heart bargained for
and I risked my whole future that day.
As we drew close I knew I would see this thing through
and I prayed I would not have to pay.

Lips just inches away with my heart pumping so
and the warmth of our nearness so daring,
I wanted to throw all the warnings aside,
take a chance on this dangerous pairing.
Mom had warned me before, don't be tempted too soon.
Remember your body's a temple.
But my knees felt so weak, I just couldn't speak.
My will power was starting to crumple.

As my eager lips parted, there was no turning back.
Now my needs were ignoring my brain.
I threw caution aside, closed my eyes, held my breath,
and the scent nearly drove me insane.
My lips since that day have known others, it's true,
but the sweetness, the passion, the bliss
can't ever compare with the innocent thrill that I got
from my first Hershey's kiss!

Watching Jackie O's Funeral

Be gentle when you speak to me, speak softly when you chide,
for am I not the one you love, the one you stand beside?
Did we not forge a bond so strong that human failing scorns?
And every disappointing day is cleansed by each new morn.

When evil thought or selfish ire, though justified sometimes,
invades the space where love should live; stop, think and then
be kind.
For though the crush of daily care crowds in on precious heart
to suck from thoughts that breath and joy that are so much a part
of everything we've always known, and that never left our minds,
somehow in stress those dear sweet thoughts are difficult to find.

I ask again that knowing me; imperfect, halting, lame,
be gentle when you speak to me, for I am still the same.
Was it just yesterday I said something that made you smile?
Impulsively you took my hand and held it for a while.
We shared a moment, stopped in time, small in the scheme of things,
and only you and I will know what music my heart sings.

Oh, anger can erode the soul and wash away the base,
and churns inside our beings and creases a lovely face.
Please, please, be gentle when you chide, be ready to forgive.
I am that one who loves you still, and must, if I'm to live.

Chickens and Leaves

It was certainly not what I expected to hear in the morning. As I struggled through the fogginess of my first waking thoughts, familiar sounds of early morning traffic began to filter through my open skylight. Ah, yes, now I knew I was home in my own bed. Living on Main Street in our bustling little town I was used to the noise of another busy day. But something else had caught my attention, maybe it was part of my dream. I closed my eyes trying to recapture my last sleeping thoughts, remnants of a dream that slipped away. As usual, it remained out of my grasp, tantalizing, but forever lost.

Then, there it was again. The faintly familiar sound made its way to the forefront of my mind and awoke a memory. I was sure now, I knew what it was, chickens! There was no mistaking the quiet clucking and throaty rattle that grew in volume, faded and started again, finishing in a victorious cackle. Then silence. As I lay there, my mind wandered to my childhood. There were always chickens, sometimes just one given to me as a pet, but often several were kept until nice and fat and later served at a Sunday dinner fit for a king. Suddenly, I sat up straight. But this was Kingsville, downtown Kingsville and chickens weren't allowed. I'd just come home from a vacation and obviously there had been changes in my neighborhood. Well, this required investigation!

I grabbed my robe, went downstairs and started a pot of coffee. To my joy, in the mailbox I found the morning paper. Delivery had resumed as requested. I wandered out to my back deck to survey my surroundings. Over the fence in the yard next door, neatly housed behind chicken wire and sitting proudly on roosts, were six lovely plump copper-hued hens. I drank my coffee, read the paper and made a mental note to check town bylaws. I was sure keeping chickens was a fowl of one of them. I chuckled at my clever pun.

Later that day, I chatted with my son letting him know I was home. I mentioned that my neighbours now had chickens. To my surprise he laughed saying, "Gee Mom, that's so cute. We'd have loved having chickens when we were kids. I think it's neat." My resolve to check bylaws weakened considerably. After all, what was the harm? As long as their pen was kept clean and there wasn't a rooster on the premises, it shouldn't be a problem.

A few days later I came home to find Peter, the friendly ten year old from next door, waiting on my porch with an egg carton in hand. "Do you like eggs Mrs. Harder?" he asked as he opened the lid revealing two of the loveliest big brown eggs. "We're in full production now," he grinned proudly. The last of my reservations melted away as I took the carton and thanked him. He bounced off happily.

Now on those rare quiet moments on Main Street I have begun to think it comforting to hear those murmured clucks growing to proud cackles and even an occasional screech that I assume announces the arrival of an extra-large.

Not long ago a dear friend passed away at the wonderful age of 91. Ralph served his community well, tirelessly working on committees and service clubs to make our town a better place. He gave a helping hand whenever it was needed. If you wanted it done, you had better ask Ralph. He was kind, friendly and, above all, honest.

Ralph lived on a lovely quiet dead end street overgrown with some of the oldest trees in the county. Fall leaves were in such abundance that bagging them for the annual leaf pick up was just foolish. The only sensible solution was raking and burning, so, in spite of a local bylaw banning leaf burning, Ralph and his neighbors burned theirs.

This year Ralph fell and spent several days in hospital. He came home and on the same day died quietly in his sleep. Of course, there was a funeral service in a very full church. In spite of his age, he left many mourning friends and loved ones. But, in my opinion, the greatest tribute to Ralph was a leaf burning evening on his street. As smoke billowed over tree tops in crisp autumn air, family, friends and neighbors told stories and toasted his memory. Not one fire truck appeared to spoil the celebration.

Now chickens and bonfires have little in common and I know bylaws must be respected. But in our over-regulated world, a soft cluck of a contented laying hen and an occasional whiff of burning leaves on an autumn evening can restore the soul.

I'm Going to India?

Last summer my son Seay called and at the end of our chat said, "Mom, will you keep next March open? I want to take you to India."

My first reaction was silence, as I desperately searched for an answer. *I didn't really understand my hesitation. After all, the only thing I might be doing in March was shovelling snow or, if luckier, cleaning golf clubs.* After a moment I said, "Okay, if you're sure. That is a very big trip."

Seay said he had started planning. It was quite a job, our party included his wife, Carena, and their sons, Rye (12), Chase (10) and Quinn (6). He added that I had to renew my passport, apply for a visitor's visa and start immunization. I made a mental note and left it at that. March seemed a long time away.

That summer, over dinner with family, Mark said, "So I hear you want to go to India." There it was again, the trip. Then and there I decided it was time to take this seriously. I needed a passport, visa and immunization, and last but not least, suitable clothing.

On the internet I did some research. At first it was daunting. To start, I needed to know where in India we were going. Seay filled me in, now I had to get moving to get things done in time. My passport was a reasonably simple task. The India visa would also have been fairly easy if I had read the fine print. As it was, I filled out the visa application and waited anxiously for two weeks for it to arrive. Right on time was an envelope from the Indian Consulate, but no visa! I had neglected to send my passport with the application. I panicked, time was flying and it was late January. I had managed to get some vaccinations, though, and if I didn't mess up, I would have time for all before our flight.

In the meantime, another problem began to interfere. My left hip had been a bit uncomfortable from time to time but now became a serious issue. At times it was hard to walk because of pain, but it wasn't always a problem. I had made visits to the chiropractor, but alas he now told me I needed a referral to a surgeon. Of course, a hip replacement at 75 wasn't uncommon, but this sure wasn't good timing. However, with my preparations complete, I decided to put hip concerns in the back of my mind. *I hoped all would be well enough for the time being.*

Post India Email March, 2007

Yes I arrived home safely, in excellent shape, well, at least in the same shape I left home in. It was a fascinating magical trip, I am so grateful to have been able to participate. The kids were wonderful little travellers and Seay and Carena took very good care of me.

We spent our first four days in Delhi. For three days we stayed at the temporary home of Carena's cousin Vibha, husband Ashok, their son and Carena's Aunt Lalli. Their apartment had five bedrooms each with an ensuite bath, so we certainly were comfortable. We hired a car and driver to go into Delhi for about 1,000 rupees ($30 CA) a day. We toured the marketplace with unbelievable numbers of people, rickshaws, motorcycles, bikes, cows, dogs, goats, even an odd team of oxen. It was a wonderful mix of noise, color and smells.

Our last night in Delhi was at a market area hotel, closer to the railway station. We were having a leisurely dinner as our train was to leave at 10:40 pm. Our driver cooled his heels outside. It was about 8:00 pm when Seay re-checked our rail tickets. Suddenly he jumped up, grabbed sleepy Quinnie under one arm, his bag under the other and yelled, "We gotta go!" So loudly that all the customers jumped!

Now we knew our train was to leave at 8:40 pm and we had to go some distance through Delhi traffic. Carena threw money at the waiter and we took off running. Our driver woke quickly. We piled in the car and tore through streets at breakneck speed, dodging traffic and an odd cow or dog. It was wild and poor Seay was so upset. I selfishly thought what a great story, not considering that this train was key to our trip.

We made it to the station with no clue as to which train was ours or how to find it. Miraculously, two porters appeared, grabbed our nine pieces of luggage, piled them on their heads, knew exactly where we needed to go, and ran ahead of us! We made it to our sleeper car with five minutes to spare, laughing with relief. Seay kept apologizing, but we all thanked him for such an exciting start to our trip. Soon we were tucked into our berths, on our way to Jodhpur.

In Jodhpur we stayed in a lovely Indian style guest house with a restful garden and pool. We all spent time swimming and, although we did sightsee, it was not at a breakneck pace. We toured the amazing Fortress Maharangar, and dined on cannon parapets 120 feet above the castle gates. Only two days before this Elizabeth Hurley had held her wedding reception in that very restaurant! Her affair must have exhausted the staff, we agreed that our food wasn't great!

From Jodhpur, we took a shorter train trip to the golden city of Jaisalmer in western Rajasthan, near the Pakistan border. The Indian Air Force was active there and we regularly heard jets thunder over us. Our Jaisalmer hotel was in the sandstone walls of a 12th century fortress. In the sun it gleamed like gold. Our rooms were lovely with windows set into three foot deep walls. We perched on colorful pillows on those window sills admiring the city below. Again, it was magical. Atop the parapets, enjoying the views, we were served a leisurely breakfast of tea, toast, and eggs. There were numerous stone staircases and I sure did get my exercise, but it was great. We visited more bustling colorful markets with cows, goats and dogs even more evident than in Delhi. By the end of the day it was an excellent idea to watch your step!

We stayed for three nights and four days. On the third day we went on a desert camel safari. The boys and Seay were fitted with colorful Rajasthani turbans while Carena and I wore shawls. We rode for 1 ½ hours in open jeeps out to the desert where the camels were kept. Seat belts were pretty well non-existent so hanging on was vital. The drive was fascinating, camels roamed like cattle as did herds of goats and the mighty cow went wherever she pleased. We stopped several times to take photos in tiny villages of mud huts with grass thatched roofs.

We arrived at a village with a school where we heard children saying their lessons. The friendly, neatly dressed and well-spoken scholars were learning English. Invited into a home, we crouched down on mats to await our camel ride. It was the heat of the day in the mid 30's, but the hut was fairly cool.

Soon our camels were ready for us but I was not at all sure I was ready for them! They were so big, even when kneeling and their visage made them appear to be far superior creatures. A little girl led me to the tallest camel, bidding me to get in the saddle. The camel had one hump, the saddle had two seats and the front seat was quite small. This was the one I was to use. *Well, I knew that wasn't gonna happen but I tried.* My left hip rebelled as I tried to throw my leg over the top so I required a boost from the camel boy. As I slid into the impossibly small saddle I was in pain, but tried to keep my composure. I said, "Seay, quick take my picture, I'm getting off!"

The camel decided to stand. I was thrown forward roughly, but before I went over his head, his front legs straightened and I was thrown backwards. Now I was up, so was the camel, but pain in my hip told me this was a "no go." The camel knelt again, reversing the throwing around, and I managed to get off. I was led to another camel with a better saddle. Again, up I went, mounting from the other side and this time it was lovely. As the camel boy put my feet through the string stirrups, I somehow remembered western movies, you know, where the cowboy is thrown with his boot stuck in the stirrup and he is dragged to a gory death? I carefully eased my sandal back so only my toes were in the string loop. *I feel so clever.*

By this time we were all mounted, each on a camel of our own, except for Quinnie, proudly perched in front of his dad. With the camel boys encouragment, off we went. Strangely enough, in no time we got used to the lurching movements of our ships of the desert. We traversed dunes that became higher as we went along. The descents were a little scary as the camel's huge feet sank into sand and they bent their knees. Forward you went, but the movements soon became familiar. An hour into the ride, on command from the camel boys, the camels knelt. We got off to stretch, kicked off our shoes and felt the lovely warm sand in our toes.

The dune here was forty feet high. Our boys seized this opportunity to roll to the bottom, and then ran up and did it again. For the first time on this trip they had space to romp and play. The camel boys joined in indulging in wild wrestling with lots of laughter. It was great to see them play with abandon.

We mounted again for a short ride before the camels were led away. We walked over dunes to a campfire our guide had made. As he prepared an evening meal for us, the sun began to drop and we all sank into the sand to watch the sunset. Thanks to Carena's thoughtfulness we even enjoyed a cocktail, albeit a warm one. Stray dogs who had followed us at a distance moved in closer. No doubt they sensed the possibility of food scraps but they weren't threatening, just shy. A good thing, we were told not to pet them as disease was rampant. The delicious meal was traditional Indian fare; lamb curry, steamed vegetables and rice.

We packed into a waiting jeep to drive back to Jaisalmer. The sky was lit up like Christmas, the stars so bright. As we approached the huge walls and turrets of the fortress it gleamed golden in the cool night air. The boys were not long out of bed and we were close behind.

Next day we boarded another train for a nineteen hour trip to Agra, and the Taj Mahal. The train ride was long but we had sleeper compartments and it was amazing how well I slept. At Jodhpur station we were awakened to change trains for the rest of the trip in coach cars.

We arrived in Agra. Although I haven't really explained this, on arrival or departure at each train station, porters immediately grabbed our bags, loaded them on their heads and set off, bidding us to follow. Of course, it was not a free service. Rates per bag were posted, but porters were never happy with those rates. If the posted rate was 10 rupees per bag, and we had ten bags, our three porters wanted 100 rupees each. At first, when haggling began Seay's white skin made him a target but finally they realized he wasn't born yesterday. They argued good naturedly but eventually saw it was futile. After agreeing to a reasonable fee, Seay always paid more. Then everybody was happy. Sometimes seven porters carried our ten bags and still each wanted 100 rupees. I couldn't blame them, it seemed like a heck of a way to make a living.

In Agra our hotel forgot to send us a car. Being a large group, we had to hire two. We were relieved to arrive at the same place, a beautiful hotel with lovely grounds and a pool. The doorman was dressed in a bright orange morning length tunic and dashing turban and inside a tuxedoed waiter offered us icy cold lime water. *Mmm*. Our rooms readied, we began the registration process. Passports and visas were checked and recorded.

Thankfully there was an elevator. Stairways in our last lodging were quaint but challenging and I did not miss the climb. As in previous hotels, our adjoining rooms had king sized beds but mattresses were only one to three inches deep. The surprise for us was that they were great for sleeping. Looking from our windows, far in the distance, there was a hint of white, the Taj.

Tired, thirsty and a little hungry, we freshened up and headed for the bar and lounge. Indian beer was good and came in large bottles that usually served three people. Today that wouldn't do, we ordered two Kingfishers and a Fosters while the kids had coke. It was lovely.

On our trip Carena had purchased bathrobes and felt hers needed altering. Since we were here for a couple of days, she asked the bartender about a hotel tailor. He wasn't sure if there was one, but eventually a gentleman arrived with a tape measure and pencil. Carena, in her robe in the middle of the lounge, was measured, not only by the tailor, but with a great deal of advice from the bartender and a uniformed employee who happened by. Seay, the boys and I looked on amused. Seay shook his head remarking, "Only Carena would have a fitting in the middle of a bar with bartenders assisting!" We spent the day around the pool relaxing after our long train ride.

Next morning we were treated to a huge breakfast buffet and a swim. We hired a car and a guide for the Taj Mahal. We were advised to go later in the day when it was cooler and afforded the best view.

The Taj was an awesome sight. Crowds were huge and everyone had cameras. Our enthusiastic guide spoke excellent English, knew his job and was terribly handsome. *He had beautiful eyes and eyelashes to die for, but I digress.* The Taj was everything you could imagine and more, so white and so perfectly proportioned, with not even a quarter inch discrepancy in its symmetry. Surrounding it were grounds fully in bloom and simply idyllic. We learned a side bit of information that in order to avoid pollution the grass was cut with teams of oxen.

Showing respect we donned shoe covers to enter the tomb. The many marble stairs had no handrails but nobody seemed to tumble. I didn't want to be the first! Intricate carvings and jewels inset into the marble were breathtaking. *The Maharajah must have really loved that woman.* We took photos, rested on lawns and crossed a bridge to view the Taj from another angle, over the river at sunset.

On our way back to our hotel we crossed that bridge again when out of the blue a wild wind raised dust so thick you could hardly see. We were in the middle of the bridge jammed between all sorts of vehicles. It was a little scary because the bridge didn't seem reliable, but the storm abated and we started moving. At the hotel, room service was ordered for our tired boys. Without TV for the past two weeks they were eager to see *Dragonheart*.

Seay, Carena and I celebrated our last night in India with cocktails and dinner in the dining room. Late the next afternoon we were to board a train to Delhi and catch our flight to Toronto.

Our last day in Agra was spent leisurely. The kids and I were thrilled when finally we had a breakfast buffet with bacon and pancakes. We packed and went to the pool, but Carena hadn't received her robe yet. When she inquired about the hotel tailor, strangely, no one was aware he existed. But after following up with our bartender, mysteriously, the altered robe was delivered!

On our last railway station arrival we had even more luggage and only two porters appeared. No problem, each man piled three suitcases on his head, slung carry bags over shoulders and dragged another suitcase with a free hand. Without a wobble they deposited our pile of bags on the station platform crowded with people, dogs, and bags. Many children and elderly people were begging. It was hard to ignore but if we gave to one, a dozen surrounded us. It seemed our mixed colors were a subject of curiosity so we smiled, shook hands and Seay took photos. People loved to see their images.

Our porters now said our train would be delayed by two hours. This was not good, it was hot and was not a pleasant place to be. Carena scouted out a fresh supply of cold bottled water and bagged nibbles. Our porters disappeared. We sure hoped they would return but, since they hadn't been paid yet, chances were good. From time to time we got conflicting news, at one point hearing our train had left. With so many trains, it was not entirely impossible.

In the meantime two little kids, maybe four and six, arrived. The little girl played her drum while her brother did intricate dance steps. A crowd gathered and the two little performers put on quite a show: handstands, backflips, cartwheels and marvelous gymnastics. We were in awe, they were so young! The act ended, it was time to reward them. We did quite generously, however, we were the only light skinned folks and the only ones to give money and food. The little performers happily ran off with our offerings.

Sights and sounds occupied our time and eventually our porters did return, asking us to follow. Our train was arriving. A vendor came by selling ice cold pop making the boys happy and soon we were on our way.

In Delhi, again bags were hoisted by our porters and we found a car large enough for six of us and our baggage. At the airport, lineups were long, but the Air Canada wicket was not so busy so we checked our baggage. Seay then used his charm to convince the hospitality lounge to admit not only Carena but also his kids and mother. It was really nice to travel with an elite cardholder! We relaxed with food and drink until boarding time.

A two hour stop in Zurich was a welcome break in our twenty hour flight. The boys were such good travelers, I even got them doing crosswords! I was impressed that Quinn was tackling the *Enroute* magazine crossword. Peeking through the space between our seats, I noticed that the answers were upside down at the bottom of the page. Quinn was flipping the magazine to add answers, thinking crosswords were so easy!

Anyway, we arrived home at 2:00 pm Thursday. Carena's dad Raj met us and took us home. I can't report on the next fourteen hours as I just slept. I drove home Saturday, and have been slowly catching up since then. It was a marvelous trip and it is wonderful to be back home. Love Joan

Mother's Day

Here I sit in front of my beloved computer. The window overlooking busy Main Street is open slightly and a lovely cooling breeze belies the forecast for another smoggy day. I glance over my growing list of "Things to Write About."

Since our last writers get together, yard work has dominated a lot of my free time. *So I guess, it was not really free.* Juggling lawn mowing and trimming to avoid golf days was a challenge in itself. *I know, golf is not a priority in everyone's eyes, but it is one of mine.* Rain somehow didn't seem to respect my schedule, adding another problem to keeping up the yard and getting in my golf. There were other interruptions, too, like my job. Although not too demanding right now, with one short phone call it can jump to the top of my priority list, even knocking an impending golf game down a notch!

Mother's Day, however, was a day I decided best celebrated by doing something I enjoyed. Something that improved my life and gave me satisfaction. My answer? I stained my weathered deck and railings. Not a task everyone would put in that category but I have always liked painting, so it suited me fine. The sun was shining, the birds were singing, my portable radio was set on golden oldies of the 60's and 70's FM. 104.3. I made a pot of coffee and was ready. It was perfect.

Three hours later I gazed happily at my handiwork, a masterpiece if I do say so myself. Unfortunately I had applied lovely blue stain liberally over myself as well. Another half hour in front of a mirror with paint thinner removed the evidence.

A quick shower and I was ready to join Mark, Joan and girls for a visit and barbecue. Before leaving, I received a beautiful spring flower bouquet from Seay and family and a delightful call from Georgia.

Later in the evening I crawled into bed feeling the result of my earlier labors. And yes, I still sensed a faint odor of paint thinner.

As I found a comfortable position for my aching body, it occurred to me that, really, Mother's Day and labor were quite closely related. I drifted off to sleep.

Zoee's Pot of Gold

The skies were ominous with storm clouds grey, black, white and, yes, even green, all jousting for their place, while lightning and thunder fought for a starring role in the skies over Lake St. Clair. We watched, fascinated, as wind whipped rain was driven first one way and then another, as though the Gods couldn't agree on the program.

Maxxim toddled to the window, no fear in the wide eyes of this two year old as he pointed his stubby baby fingers at the awesome sight outside. Every flash of lightning, every clap of thunder only made his face light up with excitement. His sister Zoee with the maturity of four and a half years, visibly jumped at each crashing sound, but she joined Maxx in his complete enjoyment of the scene outside. Their giggles seemed to become part of the orchestration.

Their grandma Betty and I were amazed and delighted by their reactions. We both remembered our childhood fears of storms, sustained by fearful parents whose well-meant warnings only fueled our childhood terror.

At last, after some time, the wind abated, the rain began to fall heavily as though poured from a giant bucket and then, out of that dark sky, the clouds separated. The rain lightened and the sun shone through. "Zoee," I called, "Let's open the front door and see if there's a rainbow." I hoped I'd called it right as both little ones headed for the door with Betty and I close behind.

Sure enough, the sun and rain had collaborated to produce not just one rainbow, but two that hovered against a still blackened sky. All of us in our bare feet ran into the driveway where the kids ran from puddle to puddle splashing carefree in the warm rain water as it ran toward the gutters in a steady stream.

Then, suddenly Zoee said, "Grandma, is there a pot of gold at the end of this rainbow, like in the stories?"

Betty answered, "Well, let's walk down the sidewalk and maybe we can see the end of the rainbow."

We padded down the street to a point where we could see the rainbow's end. Zoee ran into the street, bent down suddenly and with her face aglow raised her little hand saying, "Look, Grandma, look at what I found." There, in her hand were two bright shiny copper pennies.

We stared in disbelief at the coincidence and then Betty said, "Zoee I think you found your pot of gold, one for each rainbow, I wonder how that happened?"

And Zoee replied happily, "Well, God loves me a lot."

Maxxim, unmoved by our little miracle, happily splashed in the disappearing puddles while Betty and I looked at each other with eyes a little damp.

Sometimes there's just no explaining what happens in the wonderful mind of a four year old, but we agreed it was a shining moment.

Sidetracked...as Usual

My best friend has often accused me and my sister has agreed that I never have liked committing to anything too far ahead or making many definite plans. I have argued with them half-heartedly, but really, it is true. I have always preferred to keep options open. At times it has caused me to miss an opportunity but mostly I have found it very satisfactory.

Saturday morning was just such a time.

It had been a busy week that included a trip to ER for x-rays to make sure my recent fall did not crack any bones. I had found it painful to climb stairs. A later visit to the fracture clinic for a friend's broken wrist made me grateful I had not suffered a similar fate. So Friday evening as I climbed into bed I promised myself a lazy Saturday on the sofa with the latest crossword puzzle and TV tuned to curling.

As I glanced about my kitchen next morning I happened to notice atop one of my cupboards a large cobweb adorned with dust. I climbed on a chair and removed it. Once up there I saw every cupboard similarly decorated with webs. Before I could pour my first coffee I was on the counter with a pail of soapy water, a roll of paper towels and a large spray bottle containing a mixture guaranteed to remove kitchen grease and dirt, leaving surfaces germ free.

Making my way around the kitchen from one cupboard to the next, I was astounded to see smudged cupboard doors, so I included them in my spraying and scrubbing. Every few minutes I got down, refilled my pail with clean water and got more paper towels. I was amazed how easily I climbed up and down. As I traversed counter tops I began to think of myself as Tarzan swinging through the treetops. It was a pretty big stretch, but hey, I was actually having fun.

I opened a cupboard door to catch an escaping drip and spied never used bowls taking up space. *Hmm, I can move that shelving to make room.* That done, I continued to the other side of the sink. In passing I noted incredibly soiled window blinds. I finished the last of the top cupboards and thought, why don't I attack the blinds?

The phone rang. I climbed down carefully to find it, now on its fourth ring. *Ah, got it, no one on the other end.* Again on the chair, I heaved myself to the counter and detached the valance and rod from the wall. *I was the one that put it there but, for the life of me, I couldn't remember how it came off.*

Again the phone rang, down I got in time to hear my son's voice cheerfully asking, "Whatcha' doin' Ma?"

"Something I do biannually," I said, "Cleaning the tops of cupboards and all the stuff up there."

"Gee Mom, I really hope you don't mean that you only clean that turkey plate every two years because I seem to remember you used it at Easter."

This began a discussion of English language usage, specifically "bi" and "semi." I remarked it was incredulous that he knew the difference. I was immediately corrected, "You mean incredible don't you? But, you, being a writer and all, you would know that!"

I told him I loved him and hung up.

Now I remembered how to remove the valance rod, sneezing on a cloud of dust as it came loose. With one more venture down for a screwdriver, the blind was freed. I spread it on top of a plastic tablecloth, spraying it liberally with miracle cleaner. Scrubbing each slat separately, I listened to CBC Radio's *Quirks and Quarks* and then a lively debate on the pros and cons of cake as opposed to pie. I got into that debate so in no time I was scrubbing the bottom slat. Pie was pronounced the winner over cake and I had to agree. Outside on my step, I shook the valance vigorously and watched dust disperse toward my neighbour's house. With only three more ascents of the chair the window was neatly covered with blind and valance.

It was when I stepped back to survey the finished product, everything shiny clean, that I noticed it. The valance's patterned print was now towards the wall and the lining was facing out! *Frankly at this point, I didn't give a damn!*

I am delighted to report I have been running up and down the stairs without pain. Oh, yes, that morning I still had time to watch curling and have my first cup of coffee.

Cedar Island Sojourn

A favor for good friends, or so we thought,
four cats for two weeks does seem a lot.
But one more thing, and that's the spot,
a lakefront cottage sweetens the pot!

No cat lovers we (not haters though).
We mulled it over and said, "Let's go."
We'll make it a mini-vacation and so
fff we went, with some baggage in tow.

But first, we had to get the scoop.
Those feline four? An eclectic group!

Archie and Bunker, blood brothers of ten.
Black Gismo, so furtive, drops in now and then.
But big furry Miracle must always stay in.
His antics, though wild, always brought us a grin.

Each day we took count, making sure they were four.
'Cause what's to stop strangers when there's a cat door?

But each day at dawning, oh such a surprise!
A glorious mural when we open our eyes
of colors no painter could ever devise.
We watch as the gulls float, then dip and then rise
against those incredibly beautiful skies!

Then sadly the reds fade to pink and orange hue,
the brilliance diluted by soft shades of blue
and daylight takes over as daylight will do.
We bask in the memory and sip on our brew.

We sigh, the day passes, but smiling we know,
God's mixing his palette for next morning's show.

Visiting Lou Alice at Sun Parlour Home

The red button was beside the door frame's top corner so to open the door one had to reach up and hold the button while simultaneously pushing a bar on the door. This was how you gained access to a stairway leading to the second floor. Not a difficult process with a workable set of arms and legs and a decent sense of balance, however most residents of this establishment would not be able to manage it, I thought. I performed the act myself, not without a bit of discomfort since I'm not very tall.

I climbed two flights of stairs ignoring the handrail with a certain smugness, my new hip was behaving itself. At the top was a similar method of entry and then a long wide hallway of numbered doors. It was a quiet afternoon, the hallway was empty except for a few service carts.

Cheered by the brightness of the place, I headed toward room 212 to see my friend Lou. I passed open doorways, catching a glimpse of a gentleman asleep in a wheelchair, head drooped to one side, softly snoring, arms hanging loosely. I hoped his dreams were happy ones of better days. Then, a double room, both beds neatly made, their occupants perhaps were enjoying a visit to the common room for a game of cards. One tightly closed door was decorated with a happy little sign letting you know whoever occupied this room was definitely in charge of her "home."

I was happy to see the door to 212 open, which meant Lou was there and hopefully awake. She was, and sat perkily in her wheelchair engaged in solving a crossword puzzle. Dressed in a neat white sweater and bright pink lounge pants Lou smiled when she saw me.

"Hi, sweetheart," I said as I tossed a bag full of *Reader's Digests* on her bed. "These should keep you occupied for a while. My dad always said that *Reader's Digest* published a cure for every disease or problem known to man at some time or other. Imagine how smart you'll be when you get through all of these."

She laughed, her bright blue eyes sparkling with mischief. I was instantly glad I had come. Here was a lady who was struggling and winning a battle none of us like to think about, ending our days in a nursing home.

It hadn't always been so. There was a time when depression consumed her. She huddled inside her shell numbed by medication, confused, frightened, and totally unaware of her surroundings a great deal of the time.

Only a couple of years had passed since she lived in her own apartment, managed her own affairs, and only asked for help for an appointment or major grocery trip. An unfortunate fall began a downhill slide, first to hospital, then to a short stay in a small retirement home in nearby Leamington. There she felt alone and insecure, unable to adapt to scheduled meals, exercise and recreation.

Another fall resulted in a three month hospital stay. Lou's health steadily declined to the point where a nursing home was the only answer. Although mentally sharp, her physical abilities were failing and she needed a wheelchair. Alone, among patients unable to communicate, Lou began to recede into a depressed state again. Then one day a few short months ago, an opportunity to move into this larger, more acceptable nursing home gave her a new lease on life. She began to bloom again.

As I chatted with Lou, an attendant brought her medication, shared a laugh or two and asked Lou if there was anything she needed. After she left, I remarked on the great staff. Everyone seemed thoughtful and kind. "It takes a very special type of person to work in a facility like this, with so many different patients, some who need so much care," I said.

Lou smiled, nodded and said, "Do you remember when we first came here and they gave us a tour and told us about this home? They said there were always people on hand when you needed them and if you wanted something, you only needed to ask? Well, I have a funny story to tell you.

The other night I woke up feeling uncomfortable. A new attendant came to change the diaper I wear at night. However, she was measuring it with something, so I asked her what she was doing. She replied, 'I'm measuring the moisture content in your diaper and it only reads 75%. The rules say we don't need to change them until they are 80% damp, so I don't really have to change you yet.'

When she was finished I said, 'You know, now that I'm awake, I feel a bit hungry. I wonder, could you get me a small bowl of ice cream?' To which she replied, 'Well, I guess I could, but I hope you don't plan to make a habit of this!' And off she went to get my ice cream, after which I assured her it wasn't one of my habits and probably wouldn't become one.

She is so new she doesn't know that I am pretty easy to get along with." Lou giggled, and asked me what I thought.

I suggested that, perhaps, with a little more effort, she could have squeezed out an extra 5% for the diaper. We laughed hard and long and agreed that the new girl had obviously studied rules and regulations to excess.

Lou told me she understood how special caregivers had to be, dealing with so many unfortunate patients. Some had nothing to look forward to in their day but meals, so if the food was disappointing, it ruined their whole day. One lady rearranged her cutlery and napkins in a special pattern and was upset if they were disturbed. Then there was a lady who liked to sit next to Lou and said that Lou was the only one in the whole place she liked. Lou felt uncomfortable with this and didn't know what to do.

We chuckled about it and I said, "Wouldn't it be wonderful if the only thing we had to worry about was that people liked us too much?" This brought a smile and we exchanged ideas about handling the situation, most silly. We laughed together.

So Lou said she was going to try psychology to solve her dilemma. *I'll discuss it with her next time I'm there.* My visits had not been very regular lately, so as I let myself out through the tricky doors I made a promise to return soon. Lou's laughter and wisdom made my day.

Joan Harder

Opening Luncheon for the 9 Hole Club

Lord, we need to be thankful for so many reasons.
The miraculous changing of our seasons,
how nature springs to life at winter's end,
bringing us together to meet old friends.
To share a hug with a smiling face
and the game we love in this awesome place.
To give pause and to appreciate
the ample food upon our plate.
And be thankful for those who serve that food,
so graciously, in a cheerful mood.
For those who work behind the scenes,
and rake the traps and mow the greens.
The organizers of our league,
that can't be done without fatigue.
We ask forgiveness for one small request.
Since we aren't always at our best,
that if tomorrow we are blessed
to pass this way again,
would it be too much to ask for a good round now and then?
Amen.

End of the Golf Season

Dear Lord,
Here we are again, about to share a meal with friends,
perhaps a little sad as our lovely season ends.
But grateful for the time we've spent together
especially in perfect golfing weather.
Now surrounded by the ever-changing scene,
as reds and golds replace the leaves of green.
Thankful for the folks who work each day
to make our course a joy to play.
Who wait upon us when we're done,
who seem quite glad that we've had fun.
How very grateful we should feel
as we ask your blessing on this meal.

Lord, keep us strong as we move through life,
with compassion for others in their strife.
All this we ask in your name, Lord.
Amen.

Progress?

I joined this club in seventy-four and loved golf and curl.
Those sports were sure my oyster, but Kingsville was the pearl.
The years have really flown by and suddenly I find
the past is now the present and some things just blow my mind.
Our tees were at the top on the red nine's number one.
A good drive always started off a day of great golf fun.
We crossed the creek and valley and often made the hill.
A great accomplishment for me, it really was a thrill.
The years went by and distance changed, our tees moved down below.
We crossed the creek and valley and still made that hill, you know.
But again those years made changes, now tees bypassed the creek
and still a wondrous drive made that hill we'd always seek.
But some folks remained unhappy with the distance, if you will.
So now, I guess we've reached our goal…we are OVER THE HILL!

Joan Harder, Kingsville Golf Course member since 1974

#5 Red Tree

Trees have special meanings for everyone, I suppose. I immediately think of trees on the golf course. They are beautiful to look at and on a hot steamy golf day their generous leafy branches provide welcome shade allowing us to actually enjoy our game, regardless of our score! However, as much as they are loved, to the average duffer (and, also the pros), they are the cause of heartbreak when an errant shot caroms off one, sending a favorite ball deep into the woods or worse, out of bounds!

One particular tree comes to mind for me. It's situated right smack in the middle of Number 5 Red. This ancient monster is of the fir family, with branches close together. It is unyielding when a little white ball dares to trespass. The fact that this meddling, interfering, unsportsmanlike piece of nature has, over the years, gradually developed a 45 degree lean to the east could partially be a result of the prevailing west winds. But in my personal opinion, battered by millions of golf balls, it is slowly bowing in submission.

However, having taken aim in its general direction, always with faint hope of actually going over it and spending a good deal of every season for the past 33 years at this fruitless effort, I have to admit defeat! I'm sure that tree will outlive me.

To tell the truth, if one day I go out there, tee up my ball, and look up to take aim down Number 5 Red, finding that tree gone…what a deep sense of loss I will feel.

I'll wonder, "Am I next?"

Joan Harder

Trees (with apologies to Joyce Kilmer)

I thought that I would never see
a poem as lovely as a tree.
A tree whose hungry mouth is pressed
upon the earth's sweet flowing breast.
A tree that looks at God all day
and lifts its leafy arms to pray.
A tree that did in summer wear
a nest of robins in her hair.
Upon whose bosom snow had lain
now intimately lived with rain.

But when September came along
the robins left, no more their song.
The bitter winds blew leafy arms,
weak branches broke and some did harm.
The rains still fell but now were cold.
But look, our world turned red and gold!
The awesome sight too soon was gone.
The leaves of gold bedecked my lawn,
covered my roof, and filled the eaves.
And I was left to rake those leaves.

I love my trees, I'm glad they're there
with nests of robins in their hair.
But when October winds grow cold
I'm reminded that I'm old.
Each time I bag those leaves I rake,
my muscles burn, my joints all ache.
But come next spring I'll thrill to see
new buds appearing on "my tree."

(Poems are made by fools like me
but only God can make a tree.)

Thinking Back

This past summer I had the joy of celebrating my 870th *(whoops, not sure about that slip, I do believe my keyboard has a sticky key)* birthday. *Anyway, I will try again to correct it to 870. Yep, sticky key. Okay, I could have gone back and started over again, but I didn't. I just wish I could fix the obvious love affair going on between my 78 (uh huh) 7th and 8th keys. Hope it won't happen again.*

By now you may have figured out that I became 8 *(backspace, remove the 78, backspace and remove the 8)* 0. *I don't want to type that age again until the jam or peanut butter or whatever caused the problem is removed.* I simply will say I have reached the decade my friend Betty reminded me makes me "going on 90." *There now, that's done with and I can continue.*

Actually I had a whole month of smaller celebrations rather than a blowout affair. I did feel genuinely thrilled to reach this number in good health, with family and friends who have always made my life pretty darn wonderful.

I have found myself musing about life, reflecting on the way things were when I was a child. I always have felt rather sorry that my grandchildren won't ever experience the joys and freedoms my generation took for granted. Oh, not to say it was a bed of roses for everyone, it wasn't. But, speaking for myself, I was brought up in a small town atmosphere surrounded by extended family and had parents who did a great job providing for my brother and me. We had a warm, loving home, enough food and clothing, and the opportunity to enjoy life without much money.

If we were poor, I was never aware of it until years later. I was about fourteen when I desperately wanted the latest rage, blue jeans. My father, weary of me whining that all the other kids in my grade had them, took me aside and in one sentence filled with expletives told me that "WE WEREN'T RICH and MONEY DIDN'T GROW ON GODDAMNED TREES!"

Now, I must explain that after my mother's death, our dad became far too soft to discipline his children. So this outright statement from Dad when I was fourteen came as quite a shock and had a very lasting effect.

Dad's reluctance to discipline meant it fell to Ruby. Unfair, yes, and not easy, but somehow she managed to cope not only with Dave and me, but also with Papa who had a very short supply of patience. Anyway, we never thought of Ruby as our stepmother. At times it was complicated to explain our relationship to others but we were always happy the way it was.

I could go on and talk about those intervening years until I reached 80 (*uh huh the jam is gone*) but that's a lot of years and will take a lot more time.

Time I really hope I will have.

Time

When I am with a dear friend
or reading some good book
or playing golf in Myrtle Beach
or napping in the sun
the hours pass by like seconds
and then that time is done.

Yet leave me entertaining some
unmitigated bore
or sitting in the dentist's chair
my mouth stretched to its limits
I swear I'm there for hours
though the clock tells me it's minutes!

The football game precedes my favorite
series on TV.
The timeouts just seem endless
but at last the game is won.
A quick look at the clock tells me
my favorite show is done!

Oh, yes, then there's the toaster.
While I watch patiently
it takes forever to get brown.
Yet, let me turn my back
to get the butter, and, uh huh,
it's gone from brown to black!

Joan Harder

So time is really relative.
If what we do is fun
we gladly go for overtime
enjoying how we spend it.
But if it's just too hard to bear,
oh please, God, won't you end it?

I really tried for 60 lines
'cause that was the assignment.
I wracked my brain for more ideas
of clever things that rhyme
but I'm embarrassed to admit
I just can't spare the time!

The Recital

She strode bravely toward the front of the stage, showing little of the nervousness that her mother in the audience felt. She was four and it was obvious to her mother that Hilary had forgotten her music.

The audience of proud parents and siblings smiled as she took a deep bow. She proceeded to the piano and noisily settled herself on the bench. After a few seconds she began to play the keys up and down the piano in no particular order, on and on, up and down. The audience tittered nervously behind their hands while her mother held her breath in dismay.

After what seemed an endless time, Hillary stopped, rose, replaced the bench noisily, bowed deeply and left the stage.

She dropped into the seat beside her astounded mother and with a sigh of relief whispered loudly, "It's really hard to play the piano without music!"

A Little Smile on a Sad Day

Have you ever had days when you wondered if you would ever laugh again? Well, not long ago there were some days like that for me and especially for some people I love.

It was a cold Friday morning in December when I left my house to go to a funeral home visitation for my god child's husband. Tragic, because it was unexpected and he was only 48 years old. Even more so because he left two beautiful young children and a heartbroken wife who was fighting life threatening cancer.

I was lost in thought as I attempted to unlock my car in front of my home, juggling my purse, extra coat and cup of coffee. Placing my coffee on the car, I unloaded my stuff, got in, started the motor and drove onto the street. It took only a few moments for me to notice coffee running down my rear window, then the side window and windshield, where it promptly froze. Frustrated, I braked and over the hood of the car flew my lovely china carry mug, smashing to bits on the pavement. Embarrassed and in a hurry, I kept going, trusting the wipers would clear my windshield.

Much later, after a long day, I left my friends at the funeral home. I filled up with gas at a local Petro Can, and thought I would run the car through the car wash there. I filled the tank, cleared the trip gauge and paid the attendant for a car wash called "The Works." He instructed me to drive up the ramp, scan my receipt, put my car in neutral and sit while the car moved through.

I followed the directions, or so I thought, but accidently put the car in reverse and rolled back a bit. I then put it in drive, moved a few inches, and shifted back into neutral to move through the car wash. To my dismay, as I emerged on the other side, I couldn't see. My car was still covered in lather.

I returned to the office complaining that the wash didn't work. I was told I had not followed directions by putting my car in drive. The attendant offered me paper towels to clean the windows, at which I became angry and said that wasn't good enough.

He then offered me a rewash, loudly remonstrating, "This time follow instructions, put your car in neutral before you scan your ticket, then it will take you through."

I took the ticket, again headed up the ramp, placed the car in neutral, scanned my receipt and waited and waited and waited. Thinking I must need to be closer, I moved the car forward a few inches, put it in neutral, and went through. Once more the car was covered in suds.

By this time I was losing my cool. Stomping into the office I said I had been through dozens of car washes in my life and this had never happened before! The attendant, now with an audience of several customers, repeated loudly that, as before, I did not follow instructions, and had moved my car ahead. When I explained I had waited and nothing happened, he admitted there was quite a delay.

I lost it completely, "You could have told me that!" At which a kind young man behind me spoke up saying, yes, he should have told me. The attendant printed another rewash ticket, and asked me what he should tell his boss to explain the free washes.

"Oh I think I know what you'll tell him…about a stupid old woman who didn't follow directions," I answered as I grabbed the ticket and exited.

I drove up the ramp yet again, yes, placed the car in neutral and scanned the ticket. And sat there waiting and waiting. Eventually the car did move through the wash, rinse and dryer and out the other side.

I gave a blast of my horn as I drove out of the station. I glanced down at the trip meter slowly turning to 1 kilometer. There was still coffee on my window.

It wasn't too late to laugh after all.

Joan Harder

Snow Shovelling Crew

'Twas the night before Sunday, and all through that night
the snow fell and blew and the wind it did bite.
And I in my jammies had just wakened up,
when I opened the shutters while drinking a cup
of my favorite coffee, I brewed it myself
from a tin of Tim Horton's I keep on the shelf.
And there, in the morning, not a thing could be seen
but great mounds of white where it used to be green!
I was hungry for breakfast before going to church
'cause I just couldn't leave my altos in the lurch.
So I dug out my snow boots, a warm coat and cap
found my shovel and started, when I heard a sharp snap.
The handle had parted no hope for repair
and I gazed at my driveway in hopeless despair.
When what to my wondering eyes did appear?
A van with two passengers dressed in snow gear!
They hopped from their vehicle and quick gave a shout,
"Get back in the house, we'll shovel you out!"
I pretended to argue, half-hearted at best,
just the thought of the job and I needed a rest.
So into the house to do what I do best,
and fried up some latkes for my helpers' breakfast.
And Betty and Joe, those right jolly old elves
cleared the snow and then ate 'til they stuffed their dear selves!

Hillary, Regan and Me

The airport wasn't too busy as we arrived, but the few people there were obviously taking the same flight as we were and already lined up to go through security. Hillary and Regan tugged at me to join the line, eager to begin our adventure.

Their mom and dad were not nearly so eager to let them go. Now that the day was really here, the idea of their two little girls leaving home without them to fly off to northern Alberta seemed even less exciting. Even though they were going with Grandma to their aunty's ranch, it was a first and the two parents were reluctant to stop their hugging and kissing.

They directed a final caution to me, "Be careful, they're just kids, and there are people out there just looking for innocent little kids." And then admonished the girls, "Remember Hillary, take care of your sister and both of you, listen to grandma."

They continued, leaving me with a reminder or three, "Don't let them go swimming in the dugout, no riding the four wheeler and they can't just get on those horses and ride. Make sure Georgia realizes that."

We all nodded. After a few more hugs, kisses and camera poses we disappeared into a lengthening line. The doors closed behind us but Mom and Dad lingered, waving one last time. It was then when reality set in and I (Grandma) understood the full weight of responsibility I had undertaken. Oh, it wasn't that I hadn't taken my own three little darlings on trips by plane or worse, by today's standards, on driving holidays, and those were in the days before seat belts. But this was different. These were my grandchildren, babies of my son and his wife. They trusted me with their most precious and beloved. My stomach began to hurt.

We handed our boarding passes to a uniformed attendant who smiled, scanned and handed them back. We walked to the tarmac, and climbed the steps to our plane.

After the usual discussion about who would sit next to the window or aisle (neither of which would be me) I was automatically placed in the middle. This seemed the rule of thumb on a plane, couch, at the dining table or in bed. The only thing that made this position the least bit tolerable was telling myself that both little girls wanted to be near me. *I should be flattered.* However, at times I questioned this logic, especially when jammed in bed between two sound sleeping, immovable, and hot sweaty bodies. Desperately seeking relief from my spot in the middle I have often been forced to slide out the bottom of the bed to a sofa.

The flight was inexpensive, so did not include meals but we had a few snacks that I hoped would do until we landed in Edmonton. A two hour stop would give us time to eat dinner. There were two other stops on the way, in Winnipeg and Saskatoon, to drop off or pick up passengers.

Regan has always had a problem with motion sickness so decided to stretch out as best she could and try to sleep. Hillary had no intention of missing anything. She pulled a deck of cards from her backpack. Now an airplane seat tray is not the greatest thing to hold food or drink and is even less handy for cards. Hillary's cards were new and slippery so we spent most of our time retrieving cards from the aisle and under the seats until we learned to catch them on the fly. Happily Regan's tummy settled down as the plane reached cruising altitude. Crazy eights was the game of choice, and though we managed to keep the cards in play, when the flight got bumpy we gave up.

I remembered that I had a deck of cards in my purse, thrown in at the last minute. They were older, a deck retrieved from our mom's home after her death. For years she and Dad played rummy before bedtime every night but after Dad was gone the cards stayed in a drawer. I thought they might work for us, they weren't as slippery. I handed them to Hillary, she began to shuffle and then let out a shriek.

"Grandma, look!" She held one of the cards high in the air to the great amusement of nearby passengers. The cards, all fifty two, were of nude models in various seductive poses! Needless to say the deck returned to my purse, but not before two very curious little girls carefully examined each one!

The flight was long but all went well. Reading, snacking and games kept the girls in good spirits.

In Edmonton, we were starved for a decent meal but there were limited choices. We settled on soup and chili at Tim Hortons, which left a lot to be desired. Ever mindful of dire warnings to be careful in strange places, the girls clutched their backpacks tightly as they ate, nervously glancing at each passerby.

I was reminded of my responsibility, I needed to keep those little girls safe. We wasted no time heading to the departure lounge, anxious to be on the last leg of our trip.

Procrastination

I've sat and stared at this blank page
but nothing came to mind.
No thought of inspiration
to write of, could I find.
I tossed and turned throughout the night.
My bed looked like a slum
with papers, pencil, dictionary,
but still no thoughts would come.

Perhaps, I thought, if I get up
and go down in the night
and sit at my computer and
simply start to write?
So down I stumbled, literally,
but landed on my feet,
headed for the kitchen
but first, turned up the heat.

The chair at my computer
felt chilly when I sat.
I'd better get a cushion.
And I soon took care of that.

But passing by the fridge
I thought, I'll grab a little bite.
The fridge, poor thing, seemed
empty, no tempting stuff in sight.
Popcorn, I thought. That's quick.
It will get the juices going.
Nothing like a tasty snack
to get an idea flowing.

The popcorn took six minutes
and it really was quite tasty.
Sat down again to start to write
but thought, let's not be hasty.
You've got tomorrow morning.
Have faith, just trust your head.
So back upstairs I stumbled,
and crawled into my bed.

Flight Musings

Packing has never been one of my favorite things, but this time I vowed to get it right. My trip out west was going to be fun. I was going to a party. On July 4th my kid brother in Penticton was turning 65.

Originally we thought we would surprise John with my visit, but before plans could be made my sister and I received invitations from the birthday boy himself. He was throwing his own party on a paddle-wheel boat on Okanagan Lake. What's more he requested no gifts but lots of cards, and just to let us know, he expected them to arrive before the big day. This threw our plans out the window but we decided there could still be a surprise. So I replied with regrets, saying I could not attend. Then I made plans to fly to Calgary and from there would travel with Barb to Penticton for the party.

My last flight west, six months earlier, had been the roughest ever. I truly hoped this one would be better. I checked my list of things to take and packed carefully. I had been to a concert the night before, so was tired and hoped to spend most of the flight napping, reading, doing the crossword or watching a movie, in that order. I put the daily paper in my carryon, loaded the car, stopped at the bank, picked up a Timmy's and pal Betty. She was to bring my car home. I checked in at the airport with time to spare, not my usual style. With boarding pass in hand we stopped at the grill across the road for a quick drink and bite. After returning to the airport, we said our goodbyes at security.

Things were going so smoothly, I gave myself a smug pat on the back and looked forward to a great trip with lots of time to look at the paper and do the puzzles. I checked my *Windsor Star* "F section" for the puzzle pages. That's when it started. *No "F section!"* And no place to buy anything once through security. *I wanted to cry.*

I boarded the plane, stowed my carryon and settled in my aisle seat, which was much smaller than I remembered. I scanned my remaining sections of the *Star*, read the WestJet magazine and did their puzzle. Now, I thought I'd have a little nap. Pushing the button to recline, I stretched out luxuriously a full two inches from vertical. With my head tilted sideways, I soon dropped off only to wake every few minutes as my mouth dropped open and I drooled on my hand!

By this time my bra was becoming quite binding. I tried, without success, to unhook the strap by reaching under my sweater, all the time checking to make sure no one was watching. I knew this required a trip to the bathroom but a line up had already formed.

Ah, here come the first round of drinks and snacks. I got tomato juice. Next came earphones for sale. Again I gave myself a pat on the back, I had a pair from the last trip. Trouble was, I must have left them on the table when I was packing. However, having purchased at least four sets, I decided not to spend another cent on earphones. *I secretly hoped none of the offered movies were any good.*

Oh, the bathroom was free, so I moved fast and took my turn. Really only wanted to unhook my bra, which I accomplished with some difficulty, having just enough room to turn around in those tight confines. *Ah, sweet relief!* I reorganized my clothing.

Returning to my seat, I was just in time for the second sitting of snacks and juice. This time I chose a tiny packet of corn chips with flax (?) and a water chaser. Opening the pack I counted 18 chips, each the size of a dime. *Nope, 17, just dropped one.* Carefully now, I popped them, one at a time into my mouth, and relished the taste which lingered oh so fleetingly on my tongue. Following up with a large swig of water, I looked around for inspiration.

The gravol I had taken earlier had now worn off and I was wide awake. My seatmate, a cute teenager who REMEMBERED her earphones, was plugged in watching a movie. I envied her ability to sit legs akimbo on the tiny seat. She looked so comfortable. The volume on her earphones was set at a tantalizing level, squeaking and sizzling, but made no sense. I could not lip read, so gave up trying to synchronize my screen to her movie.

I decided to check out my address book to see if I had everyone's current phone number and address. Sadly, I ended up spending some time stroking out entries of those deceased and divorced. *Yes, I was that bored and desperate.* I noticed that John, the reason for this trip, had moved and changed phone numbers, cell, landline and emails so many times he had completely destroyed my alphabetically ordered system. A close second was Barb. I decided there was no way to restore order to this chaos. I closed the book and returned it to my purse.

Checking my watch, I discovered the address book fiasco had taken a large bite out of my flight time. I salivated watching the lady across the aisle unwrap her delicious looking homemade sandwich. *Egg salad I think, and a pickle.* And she had the forethought to bring a book.

I realized there was only half an hour to arrival in Calgary. I again leaned back the allowed two inches, put my elbow on the arm rest, and used my hand to prop up my chin, thereby keeping my mouth shut.

I promptly dropped off to sleep for a full five minutes before the pilot announced the beginning of our descent into Calgary.

Alaska Cruise, 2017 Joan's 85th Birthday and Barb and Brian's 50th Anniversary
Joan and Betty (front), Barb and Brian, Janet and John

The Move

Somewhere I read that change can be as helpful as a rest
and so, in 2017, I put that to a test.
I left my little blue house at 116 Main East.
and, yes, the noise and bustle of the heavy traffic ceased.
I found a cozy little place that suits me to a T
and though it took some time, I think it's where I'm meant to be.

The pundits said to purge the stuff you haven't used for years
but I admit that there were times I came quite close to tears.
This change of life required someone who would understand
so my dear friend took on the job of being my right hand.
Of course there were a few things I really meant to keep
that somehow in our fervor were tossed in the wrong heap!

The thought of having yard sales held no appeal for me,
I gladly found some charities that picked up things for free.
A bit embarrassing to find my sofa was a "junker!"
(Who knows, with Mr. Trump in power, it might do in a bunker!)
I learned to make decisions as I saw the plans unfold
and "precious antiques" to my mind became quite simply, OLD!

Some pieces of my childhood, though, I was still bound to hold.
A dining table, stained and scarred, with stories to be told.
I may have been the culprit but it might have been my brother
who listened tearfully to a rare scolding from our mother.
And in my heart those memories I would relive again,
to hear her voice and know how much those scoldings caused her pain.

But then I thought of all those meals with loved ones taking part
and happy memories flooded me and brought joy to my heart.
So gradually my newfound home became a cozy nest
where I could still see favorite things that outlived all the rest.
At night I crawled between the sheets content to lay my head
with years of family photos packed in boxes 'neath my bed!

Joan Harder

My Place

My own little world is a safe, warm place that I go to when troubled or sad.
It's a place where cares can't enter and my mind shuts out the bad,
where stories and poems flourish and the plots are mine to choose.
They can follow many channels, just to comfort and amuse.

I can let my brain go searching for impossibilities
like, if I won the lottery how many folks I'd please,
or, if I golf tomorrow, the shots I'll need to make
to just improve my handicap, though nothing is at stake!

Or spend a day with my best friend and wander where we please
and never waste a minute giving thought to my worries!

What if You Don't Believe in Anything Before You Die?

I can't really relate to this statement, because even as a toddler kneeling beside my bed "Now I lay me down to sleep…" was part of every night for me. This was with my mother's encouragement. I won't pretend that I understood the words or religious beliefs. As a little child it was a time to feel special with my mom who sat on the bed helping me with the words until I knew them. She taught me to add special thoughts of my own at the end, like "God bless Daddy and take care of him until he comes home, and please tell Snowball (our missing cat) to hurry up and come back, and make Davey take me with him to dig up the Indian graves on Templeton's Hill." Mom said God doesn't always let you have everything you want, but you can ask. She always liked it best when I asked God to help other people and I liked to please her so I did that a lot. This childhood ritual of prayer instilled in me the feeling that there was something or someone more powerful than even my dad or mom. If not, then why weren't we just asking them for everything?

It's been a long time since I actually got down on my knees to pray but I have never thought that it matters to my God where I am or how I do it, as long as I keep in touch. I have no idea if my inner picture of God is anything like that of others but I have always been certain there is more to my being here than just spending years on earth.

As I have wondered at the complexities of stars, sky, earth, lakes, oceans and all the creatures and growing things that surround us, I have always felt I would be a fool to think all this was accomplished by accident. The marvel of a baby's birth and even death couldn't have been conceived by a mortal mind or even a committee of the cleverest minds in the universe. The intricate patterns of our lives, the way seasons come and go, the movement of the planet, the way we hurtle through space enjoying first darkness for rest, then light so we can create, live, work and love. These are not human accomplishments.

Even here in our own little corner of the world, wondrous things have taken place and continue to happen in every moment. I have seen the hand of God in movements of the wind, migration of geese and monarch butterflies, and in rains that nourish the earth so tiny seeds awaken and grow to provide sustenance for other creatures including us.

Our minds could not have been constructed by mortals. We have been given the divine ability to think, love, hate, to feel and to hold compassion for others. Recently I heard in the news that a cult somewhere planned to clone a newborn baby. Yes, when I heard that I somehow expected it would happen if for no other reason that it can. But the ability to create and destroy humanity has come from something far greater than what we know.

I have always felt we couldn't just be here for a while and then disappear without leaving something of ourselves. And also that we have somewhere else to go, no matter what anyone has called it, heaven, paradise or what you wish. Knowing that someone or something still holds plans for me has allowed me to look at life in this world as only part of my journey. After all, why would anyone have gone to such trouble to create this place, with all of its beauty and imperfection, if there wasn't more to it?

I no longer kneel at my bedside to talk to my God but, during the day and often at night, I have private conversations with Him. I know whatever form he takes for others that He is there.

What if you don't believe in anything before you die? *I can't comprehend it.*

What on Earth are You Waiting for?

A couple of years ago I had a discussion with my grandson, Rye. He was interested in my religious beliefs and wondered if I believed in life after death.

My beliefs, I told him, are quite simple. Because I am a Christian, I believe in an afterlife. That belief is strengthened by a strong sense that all this world and its surrounding universe is so fantastic. I cannot conceive that the entire structure of life, animal and vegetable, the planets, dark and light and the miracle that makes each and every living thing tick are all due to a cataclysmic "bang."

I wanted to convey to Rye more of my reasons for loving life and feeling how very worthwhile it was, so I looked at it like this. My son Mark loves to say, "There are over seven billion people in the world and not one of us knows for sure where we came from or where we're going."

If that is true, the only sure thing we have is our lifetime here on earth in which to accomplish anything. If we spend much of that time feeling bad, being discouraged about life or waiting for the perfect time, we have simply wasted days. Days that we all know are numbered. What if that time is up and we've done nothing? What in the world are we waiting for?

And, if you believe in a hereafter, you should still be able to enjoy the life you are living. Perhaps even more, knowing there is still more to come.

But if you don't believe in the hereafter and think there is just a big black nothingness waiting when you die, then why are you wasting your only life span? GET MOVING!

Joan Harder

Windy, Cold and Rainy Saturday

I can't believe I'm bored to tears, it isn't even ten.
It's much too soon to go to bed, I'll just be up again.
I did the laundry and the leaves. They were my only goals.
And just to fill the extra time, I also baked some rolls.
I read the paper through and through, did crosswords and kenken.
I tried the New York puzzle, but gave it up again.
Made several cups of coffee, took some rolls next door.
I'm glad the yard work's done as it is supposed to pour.
The laundry's dried and folded and even put away!
I thought of making phone calls but don't have much to say.
This empty, boring feeling is just not my cup of tea.
Perhaps it's all to do with my (sadly) broke TV!

Teamwork and Cabbage Rolls!

This afternoon Betty came over to make cabbage rolls. But since that part of the job was supposed to be putting the rolls together, it was up to me to be well prepared for the task.

Unfortunately, I forgot that I didn't have rice on hand, so Betty went home to get some. Then, of course, she had to cook it. So I went to the laundry room and started a bit of ironing. Betty finished the rice, came in, and took over the ironing!

I started adding rice to the meat mixture. Betty finished the ironing and made a quick trip home to get a pair of Joe's pants that needed pressing. She also folded sheets I had put in the laundry earlier in the day while making a hurried trip to the store for ground pork. This was because the package I found in the freezer wasn't pork after all.

Now I was busily mixing all the ingredients together. In the meantime, Betty asked if the frozen cabbage leaves were thawed yet. They weren't because they were still in the freezer. Okay, so we thawed them under hot water, which took a while. Betty quietly mentioned how much easier they would have been to work with if I had just taken them out of the freezer earlier.

Finally, with leaves thawed and meat mixture together, we swung into action. I began rolling the meat into the cabbage leaves, which now were so easy to work with, then handed them to Betty. She carefully arranged the rolls in casseroles that were ready and waiting. Fifteen things of beauty just waited to be covered with lovely red crushed tomatoes and juice and placed into the oven, which was preheated by me!

After all this, I dared to declare what a great team we were! A bit of silence followed, then we popped open a couple of Caesars and toasted the job!

Joan Harder

'Twas the Week before Christmas

'Twas the week before Christmas, and all through my house,
Not a creature was stirring, nope I don't have a mouse.
The tins were all waiting, the pastry was made.
The filling was ready, my plans were well laid.
I rolled out the pastry while the warm filling cooled.
I cut out the tart shells, my confidence ruled.
Now the tart shells were ready to go in the tin.
I carefully placed them, then turned with a grin
and spooned in the filling. It was looking so tasty.
Placed it in the oven, but wasn't too hasty!
Set the time, fifteen minutes, then sat down to wait.
Everything seemed so perfect, they should be just great!

Ding ding went the timer, my heart skipped a beat
as I opened the oven, oh my, they looked neat!
I carefully moved the hot pan to the table
but it slipped from my grip and I just wasn't able
to save my hot beauties and I cried in distress
as I helplessly gazed at the heartbreaking mess!
Then I heard at the door as I cleaned up the spatter
a friend who convinced me IT JUST DIDN'T MATTER!

Joan and her famous butter tarts

Fitness

I said I'm going to get fit and just to start, I'll walk.
I'll cut down on the snacking, it won't be empty talk.
Two miles a day, yes, rain or shine, and more if I can do it.
Within a week of rainy days, I realized that I blew it.
But my dear pal still called me up and said, "Come on, let's go,
We should be glad for all the days we haven't shovelled snow."

But sports are also good for you and help to keep you fit.
The trouble is the sports are on TV and so…I sit.
Well, okay, when curling's done, the games on TSN,
I'll get right back to walking, I'm sure I'll do it then.
But Tiger Woods is coming back and it's the golfing season
so grab some snacks, turn on TV, it's a perfectly good reason.

Oh, I am such a failure when sticking to a plan
so here's my latest resolve:
I'll do it when I can.

Happiness

Happiness, according to the dictionary, is "the feeling of pleasure or contentment." What creates that feeling is very different for each individual.

As a child my happiness came from knowing my parents loved me, and having a warm place called home, a full tummy and freedom to do fun stuff. Riding my bike, playing pickup ball with friends and eating ice cream made me happy. But best of all, I knew that when things went wrong, I could run home, open the door and yell, "Mom, I'm home," and she was there. Simple.

As a teenager, many of those things were still available to me. But I worried about succeeding at school and getting peer approval, longing to be more self-confident. I was not able to find much real pleasure or contentment and spent a lot of time desperately trying to be like someone else, searching for the person I wanted to be.

Later, married and raising children, I put myself in charge of family happiness, and found myself in constant pursuit of that goal. Somehow I believed that if I could do things that brought happiness to them, I would reap the reward of feeling happy. Wrong, wrong, wrong! At times the strategy appeared to work but for the most part it was obvious I couldn't keep the outside world from causing hurts, scrapes and disappointments.

So I went back to the drawing board for many years. Now I know that, for me, happiness really depends on freedom, the freedom to choose friends I enjoy and to explore subjects of interest to me. I am happy when I try new things and pursue ventures. I know those opportunities were always there, but somehow were pushed to the back of my life.

So what is happiness for me?

I love my children but let them live their lives and make their own mistakes.

I love owning saws and hammers I can use to build a planter, trellis or whatever, feeling a sense of accomplishment as I finish a project. Or failing that, toss it and go on to fix a leaky faucet without calling a plumber.

It makes me happy to write a poem for a special occasion.

I love to cuddle in bed with a grandchild weaving a bedtime story as they lay wide-eyed, waiting breathlessly for the ending.

And how about playing catch with my grown sons, parents themselves? Sometimes, as the throwing becomes harder and faster in the heat of the contest, they momentarily forget I am their elderly mother.

To spend an entire Mother's Day weekend with my daughter. Sharing her truck cab we deliver thoroughbred mares to various stud farms in hopes that they conceive. Maybe someday they will deliver foals that will be famous on the racing circuit. Mother's Day indeed, all the time talking, sharing thoughts we may never have shared under other circumstances, becoming closer.

Happiness on Joan's 90th Birthday--golfing with her sons and grandson

Happiness is laughing or crying with a close friend who does me the honor of sharing her real thoughts and feelings. And trusts me to do the same.

None of these bring monetary rewards, but to me they are as uplifting as a cold drink on a hot day, rest after strenuous labor, or applause for a great performance.

And amazing to me is the chance to look at myself and be grateful that I am Me. Happiness! You bet!

Joan Harder

Last Minute Poem

Have you ever noticed just how often
Things creep up on you?
No, I don't mean your pantyhose
although that happens too!
I mean the many things in life
that no one wants to miss,
like birthdays, anniversaries and
meetings, just like this?
Well, lately, I've been guilty
of this annoying habit,
and often wished that I could be
that every-ready rabbit
and keep on going smoothly
through all the things I've planned.
But sometimes I just skip a bit
and things get out of hand.

So please forgive me that this poem is all I have so far
'cause I've been very busy shopping for another car.

Happy Birthday to Me August 24, Some Year

There have been a lot of birthdays in the group where I play cards
and we always celebrate them with food and kind regards.
But tonight I got to thinking that quite often there's a poem
and tomorrow it's my birthday, and I'm sitting here at home,
and I'm thinking, what if no one wants to write one just for me?
And it kind of made me feel bad, sitting here alone, you see?
So just in case that happens, I thought I'd come prepared
and I'd write a little something about how much you cared!

Joan you always dress so smartly and your figure is so svelte
that you really ought to show it off, like, why not wear a belt?
And your hairdo is the envy of all the grey haired crowd.
We wish that ours could be the same, though we don't say it loud.
Now at cards you're really clever, and you never miss a beat.
When it comes to bidding pepper, you just do not know defeat!
We all want you for our partner, so we can win the bucks
'cause we hate the way you always win. In fact, it really sucks!
And between our hands of pepper, the chats can get quite boring,
so if you aren't telling stories, most of us are probably snoring.
Oh, yes, and there's one more thing. You are really very humble
so if pride does go before a fall, you'll never take a tumble!
Just keep doing what you're doing. We all thank the Lord who sent ya'
and if you believe this load of crap, you likely have dementia!

Joan Harder

Acknowledgements

The stories and poems in these pages have been written over a lifetime. If not for the support, encouragement and hard work of my dearest friend, Betty Pindera, I would have never compiled them in one form and one place. Thankyou Betty for your great kindness.

My sister in law, Janet Thomas, first suggested and then continued to remind me that my writing deserved publication. She and my brother John Thomas set the wheels in motion, investing their time, finances and energy in this project. They typed every word, edited, proofread, gathered photos and worked through the process to bring my words into print. Basically, they put this volume in your hand, and in mine. I am so grateful!

Thanks to Janet for her original acrylic painting "Memories" created for my home. It has become the cover of my book. Marianne Kovacs, master photographer, captured the painting so superbly.

Many family members hunted down and contributed photos for this volume. You are much appreciated.

I have been fortunate to draw inspiration and encouragement from the fine people in my Kingsville Writer's group. I am indebted to Colene Pindera who introduced me to the group so many years ago.

And finally, I want to express gratitude to Emily Perkins, Brittany Peters and all the talented people at FriesenPress for their dedication and expertise.

Printed in Canada